SOUL INVASION

SOUL INVASION

Biblical Strategies for Victorious Thinking

Troy A Brewer

Second Edition

Production:
Designed @ TommyOwenDesign.com
Printed @ IngramSpark

ISBN: #

Printed in the United States of America.

DEDICATION

This book is dedicated to the Demoniac of Gadara whose story is told in Mark chapter 5 and Luke chapter 8.

I have thought a lot about you over the years, sir. I have even stood near the very cliff in Galilee where that famous herd of pigs plunged to its death, possessed with the demonic thoughts that had tormented you for years.

Though I don't know your name, I feel like I know you. Though I have never heard you speak, your testimony has preached to me and encouraged me in the Lord.

I know there was a time when you lost the battle for your mind, but for the past 2,000 years, you've had a head full of peace. Only Jesus can do that.

I would pay big bucks to see the befuddled look on those faces that saw you just after you had your encounter with Jesus. There you were, no longer hurting yourself, no longer ashamed, but in the presence of the King and with a right mind.

I don't know the names of all those who will read this book either, but I pray they meet the same Jesus and have the same testimony.

I will see you on the Great Day, my friend.

Your Brother in Christ, Troy

"The ancestry to every action is a thought."

RALPH WALDO EMERSON

TABLE OF CONTENTS

Chapter 1: Introduction: The Light Turns On........................ 1

Section One: LOSE YOUR MIND

Confronting and Disposing of Unhealthy Mindsets 11

Chapter 2: I'm Not Supposed to Have Pain........................... 13

Chapter 3: No Fair... 27

Chapter 4: Mental Myths.. 37

Chapter 5: If It's God, It'll Happen 43

Chapter 6: Nobody Loves Me 51

Chapter 7: Things Will Never Get Better................................ 57

Chapter 8: I Don't Have to Go to Church............................... 63

Chapter 9: God Wants Too Much Out of Me........................... 71

Chapter 10: Something Bad is Going to Happen 79

Chapter 11: My Kids Will Never Get Saved............................. 91

Chapter 12: It's My Way or the Highway 99

Section Two: HEAD GAMES

Strategically winning the battle between your ears 105
Chapter 13: Armor Up 107
Chapter 14: Climb the Higher Rock 119
Chapter 15: How to Deal with Your Haters 125
Chapter 16: Give God Your Mouth 139
Chapter 17: Let's Get Small 145
Chapter 18: Brain Freeze 157
Chapter 19: Make a List 167

Section Three: FOOD FOR THOUGHT

Jesus-Driven Thinking that Helps and Heals 175
Chapter 20: A Covenant Mentality 177
Chapter 21: A Kingdom Mentality 185

Section Four: SUPERNATURAL SANITY

Supernatural Sanity 191
Chapter 22: Why Snakes Don't Have Legs 193
Chapter 23 Displacement Theory 203
Chapter 24 The Road to Recovery 209

Thank You and Acknowledgments 219
About the Author 221

1

INTRODUCTION: THE LIGHT TURNS ON

Behold, I will do a new thing; now it shall spring forth; shall ye not know it?

ALMIGHTY GOD THROUGH HIS PROPHET ISAIAH 750 B.C.

"Hey Rocky, watch me pull a rabbit from out of my hat."

BULLWINKLE CIRCA 1968

How many Easter sermons do you think you have heard? I have heard and delivered dozens of Easter Sermons over the course of my life. Have you ever thought about what a preacher goes through each year as he tries to find that clever, unique way of articulating the Easter message?

See, I know every year I will have a very rare shot at reaching a crowd inundated with what we preachers lovingly refer to as "Creasters." The Creaster is a highly elusive, guarded individual who is rarely seen in church except for on very special occasions. In fact, the only time you can count on him to darken the doorway of any congregation is at Christmas and Easter. That's why we call them "Creasters."

So, here I was getting ready for the semi-annual migration of the Creaster and I was having a really difficult time. I wasn't feeling the joy of preaching that sermon as much as I was feeling the difficulty of preaching that sermon.

The joy of preaching on Easter is that it's so simple, clear, and evident that Jesus is resurrected. The difficulty of preaching on Easter is that it's so simple, clear, and evident that Jesus is resurrected. Sometimes those sermons are wonderful. Sometimes, they are not.

This particular Easter, I really felt the pressure and was trying hard to pull a new rabbit out of my hat. We preachers have nightmares, not of angry peasants with pitchforks coming to storm the castle, but more of bored and unimpressed religious folk heading to the parking lot. Like an elk hunter who mourns lost opportunities in the wild, we have nightmares of missing our shot at piercing the heart of the Creaster.

Because of this, I was struggling with what to preach this certain Easter. Nothing "made my baby leap." I never felt the witness of the Holy Spirit within me.

SO, WHAT WAS A PREACHER TO DO?

When a preacher doesn't know what to preach, he needs to review what the Lord is speaking personally to him or her about. I call that their overflow. A good preacher preaches out of their overflow. If you see a preacher who seems overly critical or especially harsh, it is typically because he preaches at problems in the church and not from what God is dealing with him about. That's a big no-no.

When I began my "carpet time," I immediately knew God was speaking to me about how to hold on when it's difficult to hold on. It was a word with some very real biblical strategies of what and how to think during those difficult times when you are waiting on the power of God. Every single Christian goes through that. Every Christian has those days when it's hard to wait on the cavalry to show up. Those days when you're doing what you're supposed to, but you're worn out waiting. That was what God was dealing with me about.

So, you know what I did? I combined the message that God gave me to preach that morning with the incredible Resurrection story in a sermon called:

"HOW TO CELEBRATE EASTER WHEN
YOU'RE LIVING GOOD FRIDAY"

That was the beginning of this book. ***Soul Invasion*** is not about Easter, but it is about how to live like He's risen when you feel dead yourself. It is about how to have victory when everybody else has written you off. Whether you are godly or ungodly, according to Ecclesiastes, you will go through times of weeping and times of laughing. You will have days you want to mourn and days you want to dance. The same Bible that says, "In all these things we are more than conquerors," also says in Job 5:7 that you and I are going to have trouble "as sure as sparks fly upward."

It's not a contradiction. It is simply a fact of life that God has made us to have incredible victory in spite of our miserable failures. Our Christian experience, no matter how powerful, is full of good and bad days. It is full of days when the power of God is obvious and other days when the power of God seems hidden. That is the difference between Good Friday and Resurrection Sunday. But, get this: **the power of God is just as real on both days!**

GOOD FRIDAY

Without fail, Good Friday is always going to be a day of betrayal, false accusations, beating, torture, pain, standing alone when you should have been surrounded by friends, and having to keep your mouth shut when you're more than able to defend yourself. It is a day when the sky grows dark – a day of despair, shame, anguish, and laying down your life.

RESURRECTION SUNDAY

New beginnings, great hope, and joy can be found on Resurrection Sunday – a day of unexpected surprises. It is when your enemies have fallen out, you get a clear word from the Lord, and doors you thought would never be opened again have been blown off the hinges. Easter is when the power of God shows up and is openly made manifest. It is when you see victory in such a way that others don't believe you.

The power of God is just as real on both days. If you can't tap into God's power on your Good Fridays, you'll never see the Easter mornings God has for you. You have to know the truth when you're living Good Friday – the truth that doesn't come from you. Living in Christ means living beyond your means. The resurrection power that comes from Christ is a "life in spite of death" power. It is the will of our God that we should know how and what to think when all hell is breaking loose. God's power has never been a "get out of jail free" card for being in desperate situations.

There is no such thing as a TESTIMONY without a TEST.

There is no such thing as a MESSAGE without a MESS.

There is no such thing as RESURRECTION without a DEATH.

There is no such thing as EASTER MORNING without GOOD FRIDAY.

Good Friday is real, but Easter outweighs Good Friday. The facts of your affliction are real, but the truth is greater than the facts. That brings me to your ***SOUL INVASION***.

BETTER THAN A SOUL MAN

I remember the late John Belushi of the Blues Brothers standing at the edge of the stage in the white-hot spotlights singing, "I'm a soul man." Dan Aykroyd, who learned to play harmonica from Delbert McClinton, would be singing the low part with his buddy John. "I'm a soul man."

As much as I love that song, I do not sing it anymore and I'll tell you why: It is a bad testimony. You and I are not supposed to be soul men and women. We are supposed to be Spirit of God men and women.

> *And so it is written, the first man Adam was made a living soul; the last Adam was made a quickening spirit.*
> **1 CORINTHIANS 15:44-45 KJV**

CONFRONTING THE BEAST WITHIN

Have you ever heard it said that the difference between an animal and a person is that an animal doesn't have a soul? People say that all the time and they are not exactly right. First off, an animal does have a soul and it is very, very much like the soul you and I have.

When the Bible talks about a ***soul,*** it's not talking about the ***spirit*** within somebody. It's talking about the arena of the mind.

THE MIND, THE WILL, AND THE EMOTIONS

The Greek word we translate into English as soul is actually **psuche (psoo-khay').** It is the root for words we use in English like psyche, psychology, and psychopath. Those words have to do with the thinking realm, and so does psuche, otherwise known to us hillbillies as "the soul." The soul is all about the thinking realm and, get this – it is animalistic in nature. It naturally acts like an animal.

Does an animal have a mind, a will, and emotions? Yes, it does. So, does it have a soul? Yes, it does. Do you and I have a mind, a will, and emotions? Some more than others, but the answer is still yes. You see, it's our soul that make us like the animal kingdom. If our kingdom, that thinking realm, is not invaded and taken over by the Word of God, we remain the same as the animals and separate from God's power. Like the Scare Crow in the *Wizard of Oz,* we might be cute, but we desperately need a new mind.

A soul man is somebody who is only led by his thinking and emotions. That makes him a lot like any stray animal running through your neighborhood. He goes after what he wants and runs away from what he's scared of. He meets every need and impulse according to whatever opportunity he strays upon. He's a soul man, or as the Bible might put it, he's a brute beast.

But these speak evil of those things which they know not: but what they know naturally, as brute beasts, in those things they corrupt themselves.
JUDE 10 KJV

Look at this verse carefully. What makes somebody like an animal? What they "know not" and what they know "naturally." That's an amazing thing! Look at how Peter penned it:

But these, like natural brute beasts made to be caught and destroyed, speak evil of the things they do not understand, and will utterly perish in their own corruption.
2 PETER 2:12 NKJV

It's nearly the same scripture! Pay close attention to this. Not understanding, being an animal, and corruption are all part of the same pitiful package. Peter said animals, or soulish people, are made to be caught. They are made to be put into bondage. In bondage, people are enthralled by what they do not understand. Now, look at what Jesus spelled out as the remedy for that bondage.

...If ye continue in My word, then are ye My disciples indeed; And ye shall know the truth, and the truth shall make you free.
JOHN 8:31-32

What is it that Jesus said would make us free? **Knowing the truth.** The difference between being in bondage and being set free is knowing the truth. It's not the truth that makes us free; it is ***knowing*** the truth that makes us free. Being set free and walking in victory is a matter of what you know.

I believe with all my heart that a lot of Christians are seeing the best part of their life corrupted, dishonored, degraded, and ruined simply because they don't know how to confront the beast. Instead of being led by the Spirit of God, we tend to be driven by terrible thinking patterns that need to be invaded and taken over by the Word of Almighty God.

SOUL INVASION is meant to be an arsenal for you to defeat the beast. If you want to have victory in a way the world does not, you have to think different than the world thinks! The Bible gives real strategies on how to think in difficult times when the beast comes upon you.

If you have victory controlling your thoughts, you will inevitably have victory over your feelings, because your thoughts control your feelings. Feelings tend to influence your actions. Having real victory in your thoughts is the key to changing your whole life. This year, God wants to get a hold of your life like He never has. To do this, He needs to get a hold of your mind like He never has. You get your life transformed by getting your mind renewed.

...And be not conformed to this world: but be ye transformed by the renewing of your mind...
ROMANS 12:2

Want your marriage transformed?
Let this mind be in you, which was also in Christ Jesus.
PHILIPPIANS 2:5

Want your family transformed?
Let this mind be in you, which was also in Christ Jesus.

Need your finances transformed?
Let this mind be in you, which was also in Christ Jesus.

Want to have joy and peace instead of bitterness and despair?
Let this mind be in you, which was also in Christ Jesus.

Let Jesus show you how He thinks, and you will have certain victory. If you're willing to confront the person between your ears and beat your beast into submission, you're at the threshold of walking blessed in a way you never have been before. If you're tired of your thinking realm looking more like a landfill than a place the Lord can spread His goodness, it sounds like you're ready to get some real Biblical answers on how to clean up your mess. You're ready for a Soul Invasion.

SUMMARY PAGE

"Confronting unhealthy mindsets"
Spiritual Beef Jerky / Truth for Meditation

1. When you don't know what God wants you to speak to someone else, review what God has been speaking to you.
2. We do not live according to the facts of our circumstances. We live according to faith, which is believing the truth of the Word of God.
3. Truth supersedes fact.
4. It is not the truth that makes you free, it is knowing the truth that makes you free!
5. God changes our lives by changing our minds.
6. What makes us like animals is that we do not know the truth of God.
7. Our minds (thoughts) influence our feelings. Our feelings influence our actions. As a result, controlling our thoughts is paramount to having true victory in our lives.
8. If you want to have different results than the world, you have to think different than the world thinks.
9. We are held responsible and accountable for how and what we think.

Scriptures to Invade Your Soul

...Because the carnal (natural) mind is enmity (hostile) against God...
ROMANS 8:7 NKJV

And do not be conformed to this world, but be transformed by the renewing of your mind, that you may prove what is that good and acceptable and perfect will of God.
ROMANS 12:2 NKJV

For "who has known the mind of the LORD that he may instruct Him?" But we have the mind of Christ.
1 CORINTHIANS 2:16 NKJV

For God has not given us a spirit of fear, but of power and of love and of a sound mind.
2 TIMOTHY 1:7 NKJV

Therefore, gird up the loins of your mind, be sober, and rest your hope fully upon the grace that is to be brought to you at the revelation of Jesus Christ;
1 PETER 1:13 NKJV

And ye shall know the truth, and the truth shall make you free.
JOHN 8:32

For God is not the author of confusion, but of peace....
1 CORINTHIANS 14:33

Rejoice in the Lord always. Again, I will say, rejoice! Let your gentleness be known to all men. The Lord is at hand. Be anxious for nothing, but in everything by prayer and supplication, with thanksgiving, let your requests be made known to God; and the peace of God, which surpasses all understanding, will guard your hearts and minds through Christ Jesus.
PHILIPPIANS 4:4-7

For to be carnally minded is death; but to be spiritually minded is life and peace.

ROMANS 8:6

Young men likewise exhort to be sober minded.

TITUS 2:6

USELESS INFORMATION CONCERNING YOUR BRAIN

Tsukuba University of Japan study of brain mass

Species	Weight of Brain	Body Weight	Ratio of Brain: Body
Blue Whale	6,900 g	100,000 kg	1:14,500
Sperm Whale	9,200 g	50,000 kg	1:5,435
Humpback Whale	7,500 g	30,000 kg	1:4,000
Dugong	250 g	260 kg	1:1,040
Indian Elephant	6,000 g	5,000 kg	1:833
Gorilla	500 g	160 kg	1:320
Monkey	75 g	13 kg	1:173
Bottlenose Dolphin	1,500 g	250 kg	1:167
Striped Dolphin	1,200 g	150 kg	1:125
Human Beings	1,400 g	60 kg	1:43
Mouse	2 g	25 g	1:13

Important information concerning your brain

Finally, brethren, whatsoever things are true, whatsoever things are honest, whatsoever things are just, whatsoever things are pure, whatsoever things are lovely, whatsoever things are of good report; if there be any virtue, and if there be any praise, think on these things.

PHILIPPIANS 4:8

Section One: LOSE YOUR MIND

CONFRONTING AND DISPOSING OF UNHEALTHY MINDSETS

Thoughts to Lose to have True Victory

Chapter 2: I'm not supposed to have pain.

Chapter 3: No fair!

Chapter 4: Mental myths

Chapter 5: If it's God, it'll happen.

Chapter 6: Nobody loves me.

Chapter 7: Things will never get better.

Chapter 8: I don't have to go to church.

Chapter 9: God wants too much out of me.

Chapter 10: Something bad is going to happen.

Chapter 11: My kids will never get saved.

Chapter 12: It's my way or the highway.

2

"I AM NOT SUPPOSED TO HAVE PAIN!"

"Your world is a living expression of how you are using and have used your mind."
EARL NIGHTINGALE

Several years ago, a young lady came into my office for marriage counseling. She didn't bring her husband, which raised my eyebrow. After a few minutes telling me how bad things were, she told me why she was really there. She said she was going to leave her husband and she felt it was what God wanted her to do.

So, I asked her, "Why do you think God wants you to be divorced?" Through tear-filled eyes she said, "Because God doesn't want me to have pain." As quick as I could, I retorted, "Who told you that?"

Before I get into this, I have to tell you I am not somebody who believes there is not a call for divorce. I have counseled people to move away from abusive relationships and, in one case, I even rented a U-Haul. I am not just some nut who doesn't understand how things work. With that said, let me go back to the question I asked her.

"Who told you God does not ever want you to have pain?" I can tell you who didn't, and his name starts with a capital "J."

Sometimes when we believe something out of order, God has to challenge us by asking, "Who told you that? Whose word have you bought as genuine? Why do you believe such a thing?"

THE MISSING LINK

Let's leave my office for a moment, fly all the way across the pond, and spin the world backward about 6,000 years to the same scene in a very different place. Under the thick canopy of the Garden of Eden, we find a slack-jawed pair of individuals with a big problem on their hands. Like a lot of young couples, they have gotten themselves into debt without a mode of payment. This wasn't about credit cards or bad credit. It was about giving the Master charge and the penalty for disobedience was higher than either of them could have imagined.

The book of Genesis records the account and it spells out the greatest act of murder ever committed in human history. With one stroke of disobedience, Adam aborted every human that would ever be born and brought death unto all of us before we even took our first breath.

No sooner had the deed been done than Adam fled the scene like a little boy who had broken a window. He knew Daddy would be home soon.

The Bible says in Genesis 3:8-11:

And they heard the sound of the LORD God walking in the garden in the cool of the day, and Adam and his wife hid themselves from the presence of the LORD God among the trees of the garden.

Then the LORD God called to Adam and said to him, "Where are you?" So, he said, "I heard your voice in the garden, and I was afraid because I was naked; and I hid myself." And He said, *"Who told you that you were naked?"*

When God asks us a question, it is not because He lacks the answer. He asks us questions to bring the answer of a mighty big problem to us. When you consider the questions God has asked people throughout the centuries, you really begin to see that, in asking, He is trying to help us.

God asked Cain, "If you do what's right, will you not be accepted?"

God asked Abraham, "Why did Sarah laugh?"

God asked the Israelites, "Why have you gone after other gods and done this?"

God asked Jonah, "Is it good for you to be so angry?"

Jesus asked Paul, "Why do you persecute me?"

Understand what was happening here. God approached pitiful Adam with two very important questions, both with the intent of bringing him to a conclusion.

Question 1 – Where are you?

Question 2 – Who told you that you were naked?

Adam could have saved himself a lot of grief by giving God the correct answer to both of those questions. "I am separate from you because I have listened to the serpent."

God could have just told Adam this, but it wouldn't have done Adam any good. Remember, it's not the truth that makes you free. It is KNOWING the truth that makes you free and until God could get Adam to know the answer, Adam's healing would not begin.

BACK TO THE OFFICE

Following the Lord's lead, I looked into the eyes of a young lady in a screwed-up mess and tried to bring her to another conclusion.

Who told you God does not want you to have pain?

Who told you we are always supposed to be comfortable?

Who told you times are never supposed to be hard?

I see this wrong thinking pattern more and more in Americans and it is something we have to deal with. When we are thinking this, we are also thinking that God only wants us to feel good. That's a bunch of Oscar Mayer!

Make a note of the bi-products of this kind of a mindset.

Note 1 – Somebody who makes a big deal out of his/her pain is clueless to the pain of others.

Note 2 – Somebody who thinks it is the end of the world if they face painful situations tends to be an emotional wreck.

Note 3 – Somebody who thinks they are never supposed to feel pain is led by what feels good – not by the Spirit of God.

An ancient man by the name of Job described folks who think this way when he said the following:

> *"If his sons are honored, he does not know it; if they are brought low, he does not see it. He feels but the pain of his own body and mourns only for himself."*
> **JOB 14:21-22**

The Bible declares that a good way to miss the important things in your life is to focus entirely on the painful areas. When we think we are not supposed to have pain, we tend to have a meltdown when the walk God has laid before us begins to hurt. Like Job described, we often do not know things we ought to know and we do not see things we should see! Confront that thinking pattern and get rid of that mess! Get this truth into your thinking:

Truth No. 1: Behind every great person of God is a great affliction.

You cannot find one human being who has ever existed who lived a pain-free life. Pick your favorite Bible person from any of the 31,175 scriptures and see if you can find one man or woman, no matter how close to God, who did not have pain.

If you look at the great preachers of our day, you'll find it is the same for them. Men and women who have reached millions and seen incredible miracles have all had tremendous affliction. Many come from abusive situations, extreme poverty or have debilitating diseases like the great Billy Graham.

E.W. Bullinger struggled with paralysis. Spurgeon struggled with depression and stress. However, they are not known for their affliction.

Preaching the gospel in power and sharing truths learned through those difficult walks are what they are known for.

Great men and women of God struggle daily with children who refuse to walk with God. Others struggle with children who are handicapped and hurting physically. All face constant scrutiny and criticism, and are expected to do and be more than they are capable of being. All have trials to deal with, most on a greater scale than we average Joes could possibly conceive.

Just because you do not see them complain does not mean they do not have affliction. It means by God's Grace they are greater than their affliction. It's all part of the program.

WHEN THE WALK BECOMES PAINFUL

Leanna and I were in Jerusalem and met a couple who pastor a church in Enid, Oklahoma. Three weeks after we got back, they came to Joshua, Texas to bless us. Steve and Emily Hula are neither your average pastors, nor are they average people. They are exceptional people and gifted in the area of physical training in a way that glorifies God like I have never seen. Besides pastoring the ministry of H.E.A.L.T.H. Church, they also work for the government in keeping our nation's pilots fit. While being a pastor and a doctor, he is also a college professor on the same subject. More than that, they are Jesus freaks and awesome servants. Again, they are exceptional people.

They gave us a personal prescription – a program we could literally run with. I never will forget what Emily told me after a full day mapping out what we could do to get in shape.

"Troy, your body is going to rebel. You have to learn to overcome your pain."

The next morning after walking only a mile, my ankles were throbbing, and my knees were killing me. The walk they had prescribed was exactly what I needed, but it began to get painful. My flesh began to rebel, but spiritually it seemed like very familiar ground to me. I couldn't help but laugh a little as I began to limp because my walk with God was already like that. It's a good thing to conclude that sometimes the walk gets painful.

JESUS NEEDED AN ASPIRIN

Jesus Himself walked in ultimate victory daily, but that doesn't mean He never had pain. The next time you think your walk with God is always supposed to be pain free, consider these random verses concerning the life and times of our Lord.

...And He began to be sorrowful and deeply distressed. Then He said to them, "My soul is exceedingly sorrowful, even to death. Stay here and watch with me."
MATTHEW 26:37-38

...He groaned in the spirit and was troubled. And He said, "Where have you laid him?" They said to Him, "Lord, come and see." Jesus wept. Then the Jews said, "See how He loved him!" And some of them said, "Could not this Man, who opened the eyes of the blind, also have kept this man from dying?"
JOHN 11:33-37 NKJV

...He was troubled in spirit, and testified and said, "Most assuredly, I say to you, one of you will betray Me."
JOHN 13:21 NKJV

Jesus replied, "Foxes have holes and birds of the air have nests, but the Son of Man has no place to lay his head."
LUKE 9:58 NIV

Did Jesus walk in victory? YES.

Did Jesus walk free of pain? NO

And remember, this was everyday life – not the crucifixion.

Truth No. 2: Sometimes feeling God is feeling pain!

The only way you can make a difference in somebody's life is to have compassion on them. Jude 1:22 says that, by the way. The only way you can have compassion on folks is to get involved in their world and see them the way God sees them. Many times, it takes pain for us to have compassion on others.

A WITCH WITH SOME PAIN

This will blow your mind. On my first mission trip to Costa Rica, Central America, I found myself stomping around in the jungle with my friend Danny and two locals. I had baptized these two Costa Rican brothers in the hot springs at Termales des Bosque two nights earlier.

On this day, we had taken a ferry into a very remote part of the country that looks more like an endless movie set than a real place. The jungle is incredible! There were scarlet macaws and howler monkeys in the trees. Everything was so green and beautiful. It was almost overwhelming. The part of the jungle where we were headed was not occupied with parrots, butterflies and flowers alone. Way back in a shack you could only reach by hiking, was a witch named Roseanne.

Roseanne was the real deal. For a fee, she would read your fortune, give you a message, or pronounce a curse on your enemy. As we were walking out to her place, I had all kinds of images in my head of what I would find. I mean, what does a Costa Rican witch look like? My mind began to entertain different scenarios of what might happen when we got there.

I spiritually began to bow up because I knew there was going to be some kind of a showdown. My good friend Danny is a Spirit-filled, six-foot-four, 330-pound, former semi-pro football player who moves grand pianos for a living. The two men with us were brand new Christians and on fire for the Lord. I sensed in my spirit there was going to be a real confrontation in the middle of nowhere and we were the right bunch for it.

Because of the thickness of the jungle, we couldn't see more than a few feet ahead, and we were on her property before I even knew it. From out of nowhere, I heard the shrill scream of a woman, then dogs began to bark. She began to yell in Spanish that we were not allowed on her property because she did not know us.

Carlos, one of the Costa Ricans, yelled back through the jungle and for a moment they had a brief conversation. I asked what was going on and he said, "She's talking weird. She says she doesn't know me, but I have known her since I was a kid. I keep telling her that it's me and she says she does not know me anymore." I looked at Carlos and I said, "That's because you just got saved and you're a new creation, bro. You're filled with the Spirit of Jesus now and she doesn't recognize you."

With that, Danny and Carlos headed to the house. A few minutes later, all four of us had Roseanne cornered behind her little dwelling.

To give you an idea what we were dealing with, she never called the devil "the devil." She referred to him as "her lover." She begged us not to mention the name of Jesus on her property because "her lover" would find out and he would kill her. She said that, on a full moon, he met her in her bedroom and that "he comes with distorted music." It was time for his visit. A frenzied conversation in a language I don't speak took place for several minutes and all that time all I could do was stand there and look at that jungle witch.

It was not what I thought the confrontation was going to be. She was not what I had imagined her to be. It was a strange thing, but I began to feel very sorry for her. When I saw her, I saw a terrified and pitiful person. I saw a woman who was tormented and bound like I could not even imagine. I saw a woman so lonely and so self-hating, she had voluntarily taken up company with a demonic spirit. She had no hope, but inside, I began to see her the way the Lord saw her. He wanted to help her.

She moved back and forth like a scared animal with her hands beside her face and neck. She continued to talk about how there was no hope for her and that her lover would be angry with her for having this conversation. "Please go," she said. I interrupted everybody and asked Carlos to translate for me exactly the way I was speaking it.

I told her that God loved her and He wanted to help her. Her response was that God did not know her and He had never wanted to help her. She said, "He has never seen me."

"That's not true," I told her. "He saw you when you were a little girl," and suddenly, by the Holy Spirit, I knew something deeply personal and I just went with it. "And when your father molested you, Jesus cried when you cried." Without skipping a beat, she chattered back, "It wasn't my fault I was molested. He wouldn't leave me alone."

I told her the Lord didn't accuse her and He knew he wouldn't leave her alone. I told her God had always been there for her, but the devil had tricked her into believing God did not love her. I told her the devil was a liar and God still loved her. She said she knew the devil was a liar, but nonetheless, he would kill her if she humbled herself to God.

Danny told her she could get saved right then, and there was nothing the devil could do about it. All four of us dropped down to our knees with our hands up as we began to lead Roseanne in a prayer of repentance. Before I did, I stepped back and took a picture of that amazing scene. You can barely see Roseanne because she is behind the brother on the left, but you can see they are on their knees. She has her hands lifted to the Lord as she received Jesus. I took that picture and then got down with them and prayed.

Do you know what touched that woman's heart? The fact that Jesus knew her pain. It was that He had been touched with what hurt her the most. I had not been prepared to know Roseanne's pain, but that's the way it is with God. Sometimes feeling what God feels means feeling something very painful.

The Bible says, "Draw near to God and He will draw near to you." The next verse says,

> *"Lament and mourn and weep! Let your laughter be turned to mourning and your joy to gloom. Humble yourselves in the sight of the Lord, and He will lift you up."*
>
> **JAMES 4:8-10 NKJV**

Sometimes, drawing near to God means getting acquainted with grief and humbling yourself before God means feeling His pain.

Sometimes, it's good to just let God take you to places that do not necessarily feel good.

A witch finds Jesus in the jungles of Costa Rica.

Truth No. 3: Your pain is only temporary.

While it is true God will lead you through painful places, it is also true He has an ending for your pain.

> *Weeping may endure for a night, but*
> *joy comes in the morning.*
> **PSALM 30:5 NKJV**

Sometimes, we are called to endure. Let me say that one more time, but this time in capital letters: SOMETIMES, WE ARE CALLED TO ENDURE. We are called to tough some things out with an understanding it is not always going to be this way. For every midnight experience, Jesus has a morning in the waiting. As sure as the sun will rise, our joy is coming.

The book of Romans says where sin abounds, grace does much more abound. For every negative, evil thing the devil has prepared, God has that much more power for me. You and I are fully equipped to deal with the situation we face. Don't run from it. God is trusting you with it and counting on you to face it like the person of God He has called you to be.

For those of us in Christ, we will ultimately see the end of our pain. But let us endure knowing the Word of God.

> *And God will wipe away every tear from their eyes; there shall be no more death, nor sorrow, nor crying.* There shall be no more pain, *for the former things have passed away." Then He who sat on the throne said, "Behold, I make all things new." And He said to me, "Write, for these words are true and faithful." And He said to me, "It is done! I am the Alpha and the Omega, the Beginning and the End. I will give of the fountain of the water of life freely to him who thirsts. He who overcomes shall inherit all things, and I will be his God and he shall be My son. But the cowardly, unbelieving, abominable, murderers, sexually immoral, sorcerers, idolaters, and all liars shall have their part in the lake which burns with fire and brimstone, which is the second death."*
>
> **REVELATION 21: 4-8 NKJV**

It's not that God does not want you to feel pain. It's that God does not want you to feel pain *forever*. That indeed would be tragic.

SUMMARY PAGE

"I am not supposed to have pain"
Spiritual Beef Jerky / Truth for Meditation

1. Behind every great person of God is a great affliction.
2. Pain is part of the process.
3. Sometimes, walking with God means walking through painful places.
4. Sometimes, feeling what God feels means feeling pain.
5. We are called to endure painful things and we must be willing to suffer through difficulties.
6. Just because you have pain does not mean you cannot have victory.
7. Just because you have pain does not mean you cannot have peace.
8. Your pain is only temporary.

Scriptures to invade your soul when you're thinking, "I'm not supposed to have pain."

The blueness of a wound cleans away evil.
PROVERBS 20:30

Man born of woman is of few days and full of trouble.
JOB 14:1

"I have told you these things, so that in me you may have peace. In this world you will have trouble. But take heart! I have overcome the world."
JOHN 16:33

Most assuredly, I say to you that you will weep and lament, but the world will rejoice; and you will be sorrowful, but your sorrow will be turned into joy.
JOHN 16:20

For His anger is but for a moment, His favor is for life; Weeping may endure for a night, but joy comes in the morning.
PSALM 30:5

Indeed, we count them blessed who endure...
JAMES 5:11

Those who sow in tears shall reap in joy.
PSALM 126:5

3

"NO FAIR!"

For they shall be ashamed of the oaks which ye have desired, and ye shall be confounded for the gardens that ye have chosen.
ISAIAH 1:29

"Don't let your mind go wandering. It's too small to go out by itself."
SOURCE UNKNOWN

My band had a gig in the Dallas area and traffic was a lot better than usual that day. When I saw we were going to be an hour early, I suggested to one of the band members that we should drive through Colleyville and look at the mansions.

Leanna and I used to do that all the time. We would slowly drive down the street, oohing and aahing at the multiple rows of million-dollar homes like we were watching a fireworks show. It was cheap entertainment and, in those days, we needed all we could get.

"I can't," he said to me. "You can't what?" I asked.

"I can't go look at all of those big houses because it makes me sad," he responded. Puzzled, I asked this forty-year-old man, "How can looking at nice houses make you sad?" Then with a pitiful tone in his pathetic voice he gave me his answer, **"Because it is not fair."**

God help us! This kind of socialistic thinking has crawled up from the depths of hell and wrapped itself around the heads of American people like the alien did to John Hurt in the 1979 movie "Alien."

There should be nothing in a godly person that gets sad when somebody else prospers. There should be absolutely no place for class envy inside the church.

Rejoice with them that do rejoice, and
weep with them that weep.
ROMANS 12:15

At the time this conversation took place, Leanna and I were living in a 120-year-old house that literally did not have glass in some of the living room windows. We boarded them up and made them look nice with Leanna's homemade curtains. The reason there was no glass was because I didn't have any money, didn't know how to replace a window, and didn't have anyone in the world to help me.

This was the first year we were married, and I had sprung a deal with a rancher to help take care of his cows. In return, he allowed us to live in the old farmhouse, an abandoned frame house they had used to store hay for more than twenty years.

The first time Leanna and I went to work on it, she fell through the floor. Three months later, when we came back from our honeymoon to spend our first night together in our home, you would not believe what we found. Because there was no heat or air in that old house, a blizzard had frozen everything. The pipes in the toilet had burst and shot a steady stream of water onto the ceiling in the bathroom. All the water on the ceiling and the walls had frozen and when we stepped in, it looked like Carlsbad Caverns!

This was the house we lived in when we drove through those gated communities and wished for things someday to come. It never occurred to me one time to hate the people who had nice things or to want the things that belonged to somebody else. It never entered into me to suspect any of those people were bad because they had nice things.

I got into an argument with my friend that day and it affected our relationship afterward. He was sad because he wanted the things those people had, but it never occurred to him he needed to do the things those people did to acquire what they had. Here's a truth for you to chew on:

If you want what someone else has, simply do what that person did to get it.

A lot of the homes in Colleyville are owned by medical specialists and surgeons. I pointed out to my friend that if he wanted the house a surgeon lived in, all he had to do was go through ten years of college and work like an animal the whole time he was doing it. All he had to do was get a hundred thousand dollars or more in school loans and work to pay them off while making next to nothing. All he had to do was pass countless tests of the most brain-racking lists and formulas known to man.

All he had to do was dedicate years and years of his life to the relentless pursuit of being a surgical specialist, then dedicate years and years of his life to paying off the debt he had accumulated while in this pursuit. After that, he could buy a house like that and pay those payments and those taxes, being sure to get a good security system, because it might make somebody else sad that he had what he had.

It is a lot easier just to whine about not having that house and suspect they got it through less than legitimate means. My friend was unimpressed. There is no way you can be happy if you are jealous or envious of somebody else. You cannot be full of joy if you have a "**no fair**" thinking pattern.

SPIRITUAL ENVY

This "no fair" thinking pattern is not just about natural things. It is in the church as well. I once heard a world-famous, great man of God say there was someone who followed him around for a while. This young man would tell the preacher he wanted his anointing.

The man of God was fine with it for a little while, but after some time it began to get on his nerves. During a discussion, the young man again said to his pastor that he wanted his anointing and this time the pastor said, "Come here. I want to pray that God will give you the same anointing I have."

When the young man bowed to his knee, his pastor laid hands on him and prayed out loud.

"Lord, I pray this preacher would be beat up and ostracized as a child. Lord I pray that as a young man he would have to go to bed with a butcher knife for fear of his father. Father, I pray he would live in terrible poverty for years and years. I pray that his family would think he was crazy and all of his good friends would leave him because of the ministry. Lord, I pray he would be ashamed to look his wife in the eye over and over again because of all the hell that will happen in his church.

Lord, I pray he would be constantly criticized and scrutinized for what he does and how he does it. I pray that he will have church splits and terrible backstabbing from among his leadership team. I pray people write books about him and say terrible lying things..."

He went to pray on, but the young man stopped him. "Why would you pray these terrible things?"

His Pastor answered, **"Because you can't have the anointing I have without going through the things I have been through."**

There are no victories at bargain basement prices.

YOU GET YOURS

Every one of us has stood in a place where we looked at a situation or an event and, in our head, we privately thought, "That's not fair." Here is a powerful truth to conquer this thinking pattern. Write this down in your heart:

You miss what God has for you when you want what somebody else has.

People who get upset when someone else prospers never see themselves prosper. Somebody who falls into this thinking pattern is always jealous and envious of others. They are always miserable.

To be jealous or envious is a curse.

I've had people want to cannibalize my ministry. Good friends I really thought I could trust did all they could to destroy the relationships God had established in our ministry. They did

it simply because they wanted what I had. They didn't want what God had for them; they wanted what God had for me. They wanted my relationships, my outreach, my supporters, and my ministry connections. Not smart enough to seek God for their own vision, they wanted to steal mine.

Since I never once wanted what they had, it never occurred to me that hell was stirring jealousy and envy in them. It never occurred to me these people I loved would look at any good thing God was doing in my life and say, "That's not fair!"

The next time you are thinking, "That's not fair," maybe you should consider this: **It's not fair that you're saved and headed to heaven because people much better than you have gone to hell.**

It's not fair you have all you have because people a lot smarter than you have lost everything.

It's not fair you're going to survive the week when over a million people throughout the world will not.

It's not fair you have never experienced the danger of battle, the loneliness of imprisonment, the agony of torture, or the pangs of starvation, when over 500 million people around the world are living that way right now.

It's not fair you're sitting in a nice chair attending a church meeting without fear of harassment, arrest, torture, or death, when three billion people in the world cannot do that.

If you have food in your refrigerator, clothes on your back, a roof over your head, and a place to sleep, you are richer than 75 percent of this world. That's not fair.

If you have money in the bank, in your wallet, or spare change in a dish someplace, you are among the top 8 percent of the worlds' wealthy. That's not fair.

If your parents are still married and alive, that's something very rare – even in the United States – and that's not fair.

If you can read and write, you are more blessed than over two billion people – and it's not because they are stupid. It is not because they don't want to know how to read. It is because we live in a world where people like you and I get to learn, and people like them don't, and that's not fair.

Why should you be so blessed when the huge majority of the world has nothing to eat, no place to call home, and no hope for anything better? Why should you get to know the Lord and walk in the victory of the Word of God when good people all over the world spend their lives clueless to the love and power of Jesus Christ?

If you went to God and said, "Why have you had mercy on me when you have not had mercy on so many other good people? Why have I gotten away with things that others have not? God, how is it that I am blessed when so many people are cursed?" He would answer you the same as He did when Moses asked that same question.

> *For he saith to Moses, I will have mercy on whom I will have mercy, and I will have compassion on whom I will have compassion.*
> **ROMANS 9:15**

In other words, "**It's not fair!**" The people of God should not look at the blessings or callings of others and be mad.

Rejoice with them that do rejoice, and weep with them that weep. Be of the same mind one toward another.
ROMANS 12:15&16

Envy and strife go hand in hand.

For where envying and strife is, there is confusion and every evil work.
JAMES 3:16

If you want your head constantly distracted with strife, trouble, and conflict, all you have to do is want what other people have. That includes natural and spiritual things.

I'LL GET MINE

I don't want what you have. I don't want your house. I don't want your woman. I don't want your anointing, your ministry, your connections, or your relationships. Neither do I want your success, your job, or even your money. I want what no man can give me. **I want what God has for me.**

I am convinced that what God has for me is better than what you have. Because of that, you will never have to worry about me ripping anything away from you. Are you convinced that what God has for you is better than what somebody else has? If not, you need to let God's promises for your life invade your soul.

JEWS AND HORSES DO NOT MIX

Did you know in its 3,000-year history, the Israeli army never had a cavalry? It never had horses in the military except for a brief time when the king aligned himself with ungodly nations. Do you know why God would not allow it? Israel was not to be a conquering nation trying to take over other nations. In other words, the Lord didn't want them looking at Syria, Jordan, Lebanon, or Egypt and saying, "I want what they have."

Israel's job was to conquer and to occupy the land God had given them and that was a full-time job. Your job is not to look at those around you and want what they have. Your job is to occupy what God has given you. Just as it was for Israel, that is a full-time job for you.

THE CURE FOR CONQUEST

The cure to the thinking pattern of "it's not fair" is the mature understanding of what God has given you. The Bible calls this **thankfulness**. There is no way I can be miserable over what you have if I am thanking God for what I have. We need to let the Lord invade our souls with the truth of what we have and how precious those things are.

SUMMARY PAGE

"That's not fair!"
Spiritual Beef Jerky / Truth for Meditation

1. If you want what somebody else has, simply do what they had to do to get it.
2. You miss what God has for you when you want what somebody else has.
3. You cannot have the anointing I have unless you go through the things I have gone through.
4. Someone who is envious of others is constantly distracted with strife which leads to depression.
5. I am convinced that what God has for me is better than anything you have.
6. There is no way I can be miserable over what you have if I am thankful for what I have.
7. The cure for envious thinking is to be intentionally thankful.

Scriptures to invade your soul when you're thinking, "That's not fair!"

For they shall be ashamed of the oaks which ye have desired, and ye shall be confounded for the gardens that ye have chosen.

ISAIAH 1:29

Rejoice with them that do rejoice, and weep with them that weep.

ROMANS 12:15

But if ye have bitter envying and strife in your hearts, glory not, and lie not against the truth. This wisdom descendeth not from above, but is earthly, sensual, devilish. For where envying and strife is, there is confusion and every evil work. But the wisdom that is from above is first pure, then peaceable, gentle, and easy to be entreated, full of mercy and good fruits, without partiality, and without hypocrisy.

JAMES 3:14-17

4

MENTAL MYTHS

In this chapter we're going to compare truth to two famous myths the world has regarding thinking patterns. Get your thinking hat on because this is good stuff.

"The incredible thing about the human mind is that it didn't come with an instruction book."
TERRY RILEY

Myth No. 1: Our brains didn't come with an instruction book.

Truth No. 1: **The oldest, most distributed book in the world – the Bible – is a God-given instruction manual on how to think and what to think about.**

The word "mind" appears 95 times in 92 verses in the singular form and 16 times in the plural form.

The word "soul" – the mind realm of thinking, will and emotions – appears 458 times in 432 verses in the singular form and 78 times in 68 verses in the plural form. If 612 specific scriptures are not enough, then how about this:

There are 82 scriptures with a form of the word "think." There are 46 scriptures with a form of the word "imagine."

There are 66 verses with the word "consider." There are 10 verses with the word "suppose."

I could go on and on. Using just these six words, we find at least ***816 scriptures*** that deal with thinking. Specific scriptures like Philippians 4:8, that spell it out like Vanna White, tell us to "think on these things."

The Bible gives a ton of solid, functional instruction on how to work that three-and-a-half pounds of pinkish-gray tissue between our ears. People who say God didn't give us an instruction manual for our brains have never come across 1 Corinthians 10:12. Use your noggin' and look it up.

Do you know why God instructs us to think about very specific things? Because **spiritually, our minds are reproductive organs.** That's why the Bible refers to your thinking realm as **"the loins of your mind."** (Ephesians 6:14 and 1 Peter 1:13)

Thinking on one thing produces something else. David said in Psalms 8 that when he considered the heavens it made him realize how awesome God is. Thinking on God things produces other God realizations. Thinking on things not born of God will produce things not born of God. Get your spiritual zipper up and cover the loins of your mind with the belt of truth! If you don't get a handle on this, you will be "birthing" things that are illegitimate or out of covenant.

That's why God gave you a manual with at least 800 scriptures on what to think and a grand total of 31,175 verses for you to contemplate. This is something He wants us to get right.

Myth No. 2: I am not responsible for what I think.

Truth No 2: **Your mind is your responsibility.**

I'm a *Star Trek* fan. I remember an episode from the Next Generation where Captain Picard and nurse Beverly Crusher had a "psychic connection." They quickly began to get on each other's nerves when the Captain declared, "Let us agree that we cannot be held responsible for what we think, merely the actions we do." It was at that point that I wanted to jump through the screen and ask him, "Who told you that?"

INTRUDER ALERT

There is nothing worse than a man who will not defend his property. A terrible thief breaks into his house, begins to take what he wants, and the pathetic coward is balled up in his bed with the covers over his head. His wife comes to him and says, "Why did you let that stranger ransack our home?" The coward answers, "I can't be held responsible for who comes in here." Would that fly with your wife? Not if she has any sense. No, it is not your fault you're being invaded; however, it is your fault that you don't defend your property. You fight for what God has trusted you with, especially your thinking. **You are held responsible for what you think.** How you think shapes who you are. You are responsible for who you are.

For as he thinketh in his heart, so is he…
PROVERBS 23:7

The mind of each man is the man himself.
MARCUS TULLIUS CICERO

I love what Abraham Lincoln said: "People are just about as happy as they make up their minds to be."

Make up your mind the way your mom taught you to make up your bed. Straighten it out! **You are responsible for defending your mind against random thoughts that do not glorify the Lord.** You wouldn't let ungodly things into your home, yet you let things into your head you would never allow into any piece of property you own. You are responsible for defending your thinking against mental intrusions.

For the weapons of our warfare are not carnal, but mighty through God to the pulling down of strongholds; Casting down imaginations, and every high thing that exalteth itself against the knowledge of God and bringing into captivity every thought to the obedience of Christ; And having in a readiness to revenge all disobedience, when your obedience is fulfilled.
2 CORINTHIANS 10:4-6

Pick up your gun – the Word – and blast that devil from hell who is breaking into your head. Don't ball up in your bed and let him take away what belongs to you.

Defend yourself! It makes God sorry you were even born when you refuse to protect your mind. Read why God wiped out the people of Noah's generation.

> *And God saw that the wickedness of man was great in the earth, and that* every imagination of the thoughts *of his heart was only evil continually. And it repented the LORD that He had made man on the earth, and it grieved Him at His heart. And the LORD said, I will destroy man whom I have created from the face of the earth...*
>
> **GENESIS 6:5-7**

He judged their thoughts because thoughts lead to actions – always! A sure-fire way to grieve God and bring His wrath down upon you is to refuse to be held responsible for what and how you think. It just doesn't fly.

SUMMARY PAGE

"Mental Myths"
Spiritual Beef Jerky / Truth for Meditation

1. God did give us an instruction manual for our heads and it is our responsibility to know what it says.
2. We are responsible for what and how we think.
3. Refusing to conquer our thinking is rebellion against God and it brings judgment.

Scriptures to invade your soul when thinking, "I'm not responsible for what I think."

For as he thinketh in his heart, so is he…
PROVERBS 23:7

For the weapons of our warfare are not carnal, but mighty through God to the pulling down of strongholds; Casting down imaginations, and every high thing that exalteth itself against the knowledge of God and bringing into captivity every thought to the obedience of Christ; And having in a readiness to revenge all disobedience, when your obedience is fulfilled.
2 CORINTHIANS 10:4-6

And God saw that the wickedness of man was great in the earth, and that every imagination of the thoughts of his heart *was only evil continually.*
GENESIS 6:5

5

"IF IT IS A GOD THING, IT WILL HAPPEN"

"The mind has exactly the same power as the hands: not merely to grasp the world, but to change it."
COLIN WILSON

You're sitting in a cold wooden chair and the jury has just come in after only twenty minutes of deliberation. That's not good because your life is on the line.

You were not prepared for your case. You didn't have a good defense. There was no strategy. When it came down to your life or death, the only thing you said into the microphone was, "If it's God's will, I will succeed. If it is not God's will, I will fail."

As the jury foreman begins to read the verdict, you know what he's going to say before he even reads it. You're going to die!

Here's what's real: you would never go into a courtroom without a plan and a strategy to succeed, especially with your life on the line. While that is true, many Christians go into marriage, parenting, or their careers without a strategy or any kind of plan while truly believing, "If God is in it, I will succeed. If He's not, then I won't."

That's a classic messed up way to think. If this is you, your head is in need of a serious soul invasion.

GOD GETS DISAPPOINTED

First of all, God doesn't say *if* He wants you to prosper you will. That's crazy. God wants everyone to prosper. God hates for anybody to fail.

The Lord is not slack concerning His promise,
as some men count slackness; but is longsuffering
to us-ward, not willing that any should perish,
but that all should come to repentance.
2 PETER 3:9

The fact of the matter is, there has never been anyone more let down than God Almighty. There have been billions of people He has set up for success who were never able to grab hold of it. There have been billions of times when great things could have happened that did not. Not just once or twice, but this has happened every day in the history of humanity.

I guarantee many things have not happened that He wanted to happen, and those things have broken His heart. It reminds me of a time when Jesus sat on the Mount of Olives overlooking Jerusalem. Great big tears streamed down His face as He looked upon those ancient walls of His holy city.

"O Jerusalem, Jerusalem, you who kill the prophets
and stone those sent to you, how often I have longed
to gather your children together, as a hen gathers her
chicks under her wings, but you were not willing."
MATTHEW 23:37

He was saying, "I wanted to do such great things with you, and for you, but you just wouldn't let me."

You see, the rule is not if God wants it to happen it will happen. The rule is that if God wants it to happen **and you get with His program**, it will happen.

You don't prosper and have success just because God wants you to. You prosper and have success when you're committed to what God has for you.

This Book of the Law (the word of God) shall not depart from your mouth, but you shall meditate in it day and night, that you may observe to do according to all that is written in it. For then you will make your way prosperous, and then you will have good success.

JOSHUA 1:8

It takes a day and night commitment to have good success. It takes great diligence.

He who has a slack hand becomes poor, but the hand of the diligent makes rich.

PROVERBS 10:4

Success comes from diligence. To be diligent means to be determined, eager and decisive. Laziness and passiveness are the same thing, neither of which are connected to success.

The vision God has given you can only be achieved by strategic and aggressive action.

Let's look at someone who just laid around and said, "If God wants it to happen it will." You will find him in the book of Proverbs.

I went by the field of the lazy man, and by the vineyard of the man devoid of understanding; And there it was, all overgrown with thorns; Its surface was covered with nettles; Its stone wall was broken down. When I saw it, I considered it well; I looked on it and received instruction: A little sleep, a little slumber, A little folding of the hands to rest. So shall your poverty come like a prowler, and your need like an armed man.

PROVERBS 24:30-34

Just hoping that good things would happen without any action caused this guy to be poor.

WHAT'S WRONG WITH THE LAZY (PASSIVE) MAN'S VINEYARD?

1. It was overgrown with thorns.

It had become painful instead of being sweet and valuable. I know a lot of marriages like that because they won't take any kind of decisive action. They just continue on as usual and hope things will get better somehow, but their marriage becomes full of thorns.

2. Its surface was covered with nettles.

It had grown ugly and was no longer pleasant to look at. I have known a lot of people whose finances were a lot like this. They just sat around saying, "If God wants me to prosper I will," while their credit and debt became something they couldn't face or even think about.

3. Its walls were broken down.

No longer protected, it was vulnerable to anything that wanted to come in and steal from it or destroy it. I have seen a lot of families that looked just like that simply because the parents wouldn't get up and take decisive action.

All of these things are true of a passive man's marriage, his relationship with his children, his finances, his walk with God, his career, his body, and especially his vision.

"If it is God, it'll happen. If it is not God, it will not happen" is a religious excuse for not wanting to get off the couch. It's a pious justification for being irrelevant and not being the person God has called us to be.

THE OLD MAN SPEAKS

There is a story in the book of Acts about one of the great Jewish leaders of Jesus' day by the name of Gamaliel. The Bible says he was respected by all the people and Paul himself went to his Bible college before Jesus knocked him off his high horse.

When several of the apostles were thrown into jail for preaching the Gospel, the counsel of the Jews had a hard time deciding what to do with them. As a result, Gamiliel took the floor and here is what he said:

> *"Men of Israel, take heed to yourselves what you intend to do regarding these men. For some time ago Theudas rose up, claiming to be somebody. A number of men, about four hundred, joined him. He was slain, and all who obeyed him were scattered and came to nothing. After this man, Judas of Galilee rose up in the days of the census and drew away many people after him. He also perished, and all who obeyed him were dispersed. And now I say to you, keep away from these men and let them alone;* for if this plan or this work is of men, it will come to nothing; but if it is of God, you cannot overthrow it — *lest you even be found to fight against God."*
>
> **ACTS 5:35-39**

This sounds like a great answer, but the Word *never* says that. Here's what's real: This was the thinking among Israel's top leadership in those days and look at what Jesus said about this same bunch:

> *"Woe unto you, scribes and Pharisees, hypocrites! For ye compass sea and land to make one proselyte, and when he is made, ye make him twofold more the child of hell than yourselves."*
>
> **MATTHEW 23:15**

This is the classic wrong thinking of religious people who sit on their blessed assurance while the world around them goes to hell. It is the speech of a man who refuses to take decisive action and has a policy of not getting involved.

Quoting these words spoken by a Pharisee, pastors and church leadership sit around today with the great respect of their congregation saying, "If God wants us to have a revival we will. If not, we won't." Meanwhile, they have no idea how irrelevant, out-of-date, and insignificant they are to the very people God has called them to make an impact upon.

HERE'S THE TRUTH

Vision is achieved through strategic action and aggressive moves.

Have a God-given plan. Get a God-given strategy. Get some God-given courage and grace to make some things happen to achieve your God-given vision. You are supposed to put a lot of thought and work into the vision God has given you.

God is into strategy and He cannot stand it when we blame Him when things don't pan out, ministries are not effective, or people we trust don't live up to our expectations.

SUMMARY PAGE

"If it's God, it'll happen"
Spiritual Beef Jerky / Truth for Meditation

1. God wants you to prosper, but you never will until you get with His program.
2. The Bible says it takes day and night commitment to have success. (Joshua 1:8)
3. The vision God has given you can only be achieved by strategic action and aggressive moves on your part.

Scriptures to invade your soul when you're thinking, "If it's a God thing, it will happen."

The Lord is not slack concerning His promise,
as some men count slackness; but is longsuffering
to us-ward, not willing that any should perish,
but that all should come to repentance.

2 PETER 3:9

This Book of the Law (the word of God) shall not
depart from your mouth, but you shall meditate in it
day and night, that you may observe to do according to
all that is written in it. For then you will make your
way prosperous, and then you will have good success.

JOSHUA 1:8

He who has a slack hand becomes poor,
but the hand of the diligent makes rich.

PROVERBS 10:4

6

"NOBODY LOVES ME!"

But God proves His love for us in that while we still were sinners Christ died for us.
ROMANS 5:8

The eye sees only what the mind is prepared to comprehend.
HENRI BERGSON

Every single Christian in the world, no matter how loved, has to deal with this thought pattern at different times during their life. If you are smart enough to realize you are greatly loved by God and whatever circle of people you are blessed with, the devil will still try to get you to focus on the one or two dummies who should love you but do not.

There may be people in your life who should love you but, no matter what you do, they just will not. You may be incredibly disappointed because you are on the bad side of someone you hoped would respect you.

Let me ask you this: why should your attention be given to those one or two people who don't care about you when there are other people who obviously do love you and respect you?

When our mental attention is devoted to those who do not love us, our lives become afflicted in every area.

There's a crossed-eyed woman in the Bible that her daddy called a "wild cow." Leah, as beautiful as it sounds in English, is not so pretty in Hebrew unless wild cow sounds pretty to you.

For every sideways look and hurtful remark poor Leah received, her sister, Rachel, received ten praises for her beauty and grace. Her father, Laban, was so convinced no one would ever marry Leah he conned a con man by the name of Jacob into giving her his ring.

When Jacob realized his bride was Leah and not Rachel, Laban sprung a deal that landed both of his daughters in the honeymoon tent of Jacob. Let me tell you this: Jacob and Rachel hated Leah for her intrusion into their marriage, even though it wasn't her fault. She became the ex-wife that never left. Jacob would visit her from time to time, but he never really wanted anything to do with her.

Leah hoped she would make her husband love her, but the only place she ever filled in Jacob's heart was to be a plaything for him to abuse. She was good enough to sleep with, but not good enough to treat right. Her entire life revolved around the fact that the people who should have loved her refused to love her. She was not respected by the man who should have respected her. That was Leah's life.

Despite his disdain, it wasn't very long before she started bearing Jacob's children. Read what the Bible says.

> *And Leah conceived, and bore a son, and she called his name Reuben: for she said, "Surely the LORD hath looked upon my affliction;* now therefore my husband will love me."
>
> **GENESIS 29:32**

Reuben means "the man" or "it's a boy." She was convinced Jacob would love her after she gave him a son, but it just didn't happen. In fact, Rachel hated her all the more because Leah was giving birth and Rachel was having problems getting pregnant.

> *And she conceived again, and bore a son; and said,* "Because the LORD hath heard that I was hated, *he hath therefore given me this son also: and she called his name Simeon."*
>
> **GENESIS 29:33**

Simeon means "hearing" or "God hears." She just knew that now God was going to answer her prayer and her husband was going to love her. Again, it didn't happen.

> *And she conceived again, and bore a son; and said, "Now this time* will my husband be joined unto me, *because I have born him three sons: therefore, was his name called Levi."*
> **GENESIS 29:34**

Levi means "joined" or "hooked up." She wanted so badly to be united with her husband. Her heart's desire was to be loved like a real wife, not like a cheap prostitute. Still, it didn't happen. However, something different did happen after this birth, and it didn't happen in Jacob or Rachel. It happened inside Leah's thinking.

One day, in the midst of her misery, a new light began to dawn on Leah. She had an epiphany. She got an awesome revelation. Look at what the next verse says:

> *And she conceived again, and bore a son: and she said,* "Now will I praise the Lord: *therefore, she called his name Judah"; and* left bearing.
> **GENESIS 29:35**

Judah means "praise." She quit mourning over the lack of love from Jacob and even her sister Rachel. Instead, she started praising God for the fact that He loved her. She learned how to ignore Jacobs's lack of love and started focusing on the fact that she was loved by somebody bigger than Jacob.

PRAISING GOD THAT HE LOVES YOU IS THE CURE FOR THE THINKING PATTERN OF "NOBODY LOVES ME."

Do you really know how loved you are by the only One who really matters? His name is Jesus Christ and Zechariah 2:8 says that whoever touches you touches "the apple of His eye." That's the pupil or the untouchable part of His eye.

Jeremiah 29:11 says that when God thinks about you, He thinks thoughts of peace and plans to bring you to an expected end – a certain outcome, or specific plan for your life.

Revelation 1:6 says that when God sees you, He doesn't see you the way everybody else sees you. Rather, He sees you as a king and a priest. Daddy calls you royalty! Your spiritual Father sees you as a monarch and a sovereign. If He's got a wallet, your picture is in it. If God has a refrigerator, your accomplishments are displayed all over it!

He embarrasses the devil by bragging on you the way He bragged on Job. Do you know that?

GET OUT OF MY BED AND OUT OF MY HEAD!

The last part of that verse says Leah quit bearing children for Jacob. That means she gave him the left foot of fellowship and Jacob no longer had intimate access to her. Leah told Jacob, "No more, big boy." She quit crying about the fact Jacob didn't love her and started praising God for the fact that He did. When she changed her thinking, it changed everything!

Leah woke up one day and said, "I refuse to let people who don't love me birth something through me." She finally decided she was going to allow God to birth something through her. It was through Judah – her praise – that Jesus was born.

You've never heard of the Lion of the Tribe of Rueben, Simeon, or Levi. Jesus is known forever as the Lion of the Tribe of Judah. Jesus showed up in the messed-up life of a cross-eyed wild cow when she quit focusing on folks who didn't love her and started praising God because He did love her. It works the same way with you and me.

And think about this: Though God created and loves each one of us enough to sacrifice His Son – part of Himself – on a cross to save us from the Godless mess we made, many of us do not love Him. It's called free will and each of us has been given it as a gift because love requires freedom. If God can't make His own children love Him – and He is amazingly good – what makes you and I think we can make people love us?

SUMMARY PAGE

"Nobody loves me"
Spiritual Beef Jerky / Truth for Meditation

1. When our mental attention is devoted to those who do not love us, our lives become afflicted in every area.
2. If the devil cannot get you to believe nobody loves you, he will make you focus on the one or two dummies who do not.
3. If God cannot make people love Him, what makes you think you can make people love you?
4. Getting a real revelation of the love God has for you, accompanied by verbal praise to Him for that love, is the cure to the "nobody loves me" blues.
5. There is no way I can be miserable over not being loved if I am praising God for how much I am loved.
6. Jesus did not show up through Leah until she started praising Him.

Scriptures to invade your soul when you're thinking, "Nobody loves me"

For while we were still weak, at the right time, Christ died for the ungodly. Indeed, rarely will anyone die for a righteous person—though perhaps for a good person someone might actually dare to die. But God proves His love for us in that, while we still were sinners, Christ died for us.

ROMANS 5:6-8

Greater love hath no man than this, that a man lay down his life for his friends.

JOHN 15:13

One more note. You can't truly love other people until you understand that God loves you. The greater your revelation of how God loves you, the greater your capacity to demonstrate His love to others.

Evangeline Booth, the daughter of the founder of the Salvation Army, had a real revelation of the Jesus kind of love. She sat in a filthy slum one day cleaning the sores of a drunk woman when a friend said, "I wouldn't do that for a million dollars."

Evangeline Booth replied, "Neither would I."

She understood what love was all about.

That's the way Jesus loves you.

7

THINGS WILL NEVER GET BETTER

THE FIGHT AGAINST DEPRESSION

"We ought to mind our thoughts, for if they turn out to be our enemies they will be too many to fight and will drag us down to ruin."
CHARLES SPURGEON

The devil loves to exploit the issue of depression. Some people are much more prone than others to have this kind of mental malfunction. However, what's real is that every single one of us have to make a stand against it. Let's talk about that.

A SAD DISAPPOINTMENT

Let me tell you something about the cosmic punk you and I call the devil. He's extremely evil with a capital "D," but that does not make him extremely big or extremely powerful. If you fight him on your turf, he will eat you for lunch. But, if you fight him on the turf Jesus gives you, he is seen as he truly is – a schoolyard bully who can be dealt with.

The reason he works in darkness is because he doesn't want you to know how pathetic he really is. In the dark, we envision him to be a horrible, undefeatable, brilliant strategist – a mass of muscle, bone, and teeth. But shine the spotlight of truth onto him. The truth about Satan is found in the book of Isaiah.

"Those who see you stare at you, they ponder your fate: "Is this the man who shook the earth and made kingdoms tremble, the man who made the world a desert, who overthrew its cities and would not let his captives go home?"
ISAIAH 14:16-17

The fact is, we give him a lot more credit than he deserves. He is not a brilliant strategist or even a brutal general. He is a bully and a child molester who picks on weak people in their weakest areas during the weakest times of their lives. He is merely an evil opportunist. He is a lot like the punk kids in the bad part of your town who look for unlocked doors on parked cars.

Is he a threat and something you need to be aware of? Absolutely yes. Is he a terrible force that is undefeatable? Absolutely not.

> *Be sober, be vigilant; because your adversary the devil, as a roaring lion, walketh about, seeking whom he may devour.*
> **1 PETER 5:8**

Not whom he "*can*," but rather, whom he "*may*" devour. The devil might be *like* a roaring lion but only in the sense that he is looking for an opportunity – an unlocked door – to pounce. He needs our permission to attack, so when he says, "May I?" tell him, "No."

UNIDENTIFIED FLYING THOUGHTS

Satan and his demonic forces have been with you since you were little, so they can exactly imitate your thoughts. They sit beside your head and whisper things you and I mistake as our

own thoughts. Many times, when darkness speaks, it sounds like those thoughts are our own. Don't believe everything you think.

"Things will never get better," they whisper.

"My mess is never going to change," you answer under your breath.

The next time you begin to say or think that, you need to ask yourself, "Who told me that?"

Have you not heard the 23rd Psalm? Of course, you have. The Word declares that the Lord is your shepherd and He is going to make you to lie down in green pastures. It is Him who leads you beside still waters.

Do you know what a green pasture is? It is a safe place. That's why you can lay down there. It is a feeding place. It is your shepherd's plan to take you to some new places – places full of life and safety. In these places, you are going to be fed in ways you never have been before. Those are His plans, so follow Him.

Do you know what still waters are? They are a peaceful place. That is why the next verse says, "He restores my soul." That means He puts your mind back together.

God is leading you into better places where you can have supernatural sanity – where things make sense. It is never God who tells you things will never get better. Every time God shows up, He gives you hope for something better.

In the book of Hebrews, God Almighty is known as the "God of better things." Romans chapter 4:18 talks

about Abraham who, when it came to having a son and leaving a lasting legacy, had thought for 50 years it was never going to happen. It was never going to get any better.

God showed up and all that changed.

> *Who against hope believed in hope, that he might become the father of many nations, according to that which was spoken, so shall thy seed be. And being not weak in faith, he considered not his own body now dead, when he was about one hundred years old, neither yet the deadness of Sarah's womb: He staggered not at the promise of God through unbelief; but was strong in faith, giving glory to God...*
> **ROMANS 4:18-20**

So, here is the scriptural principle for folks who tend to think things are never going to get any better:

Knowing the promises of God for your life is the answer to depression or the thinking pattern of "things will never get better."

You cannot buy into that lie if you are hanging onto very specific promises. You need hope. You need God to whisper some promises into your life. You need to hang onto those promises and refuse to believe your situation is not going to get better. **If you are following God, you are following Him into better places.** Maybe things are not getting *easier*, but things are definitely getting *better*. Easier is never better. Better is also harder. Don't confuse the two.

Don't look for something easier. Look for something better. Don't think things will never get better. Know the promises of

God for your life and say to hell with the devil who says nothing is going to get better.

What promises do you hold onto when the devil begins to whisper his lies? Do you have what I call "an ***inventory of hope***?" If you don't, how can you seek God for His promises?

I would encourage you to have a God-given list of promises from the throne that the Lord has given you in your times of radically seeking Him. (See "Make a list" in section two) Write them down, hang onto them, profess them, and stand on them. Things are getting better and the spirit of depression can be ordered to leave.

Your doomsday is not inevitable. Jesus is alive!

SUMMARY PAGE

"Things will never get better"
Spiritual Beef Jerky / Truth for Meditation

1. The next time you begin to think things will never get better, ask yourself, "Who told me that?"
2. There is always hope in Jesus. In the book of Hebrews, God is known as the "God of better things."
3. Knowing the promises of God for your life is the answer to the thinking pattern of "things will never get better."
4. Better will not be easier, but it will be better. Refuse to settle for easier when you can have better.
5. Hope: a wish or desire accompanied by confident expectation of its fulfillment.
6. You should always keep a mental inventory of hope. Write down a list of reasons for confident expectation and keep it on hand.

"...And be ready always to make a case
to everyone who asks you for a reason
concerning the hope which is in you..."
1 PETER 3:15

Scriptures to invade your soul when you're thinking, "Things will never get better"

For I know the plans I have for you," declares the LORD, "plans to prosper you and not to harm you, plans to give you hope and a future."

JEREMIAH 29:11

It is good that a man should both hope and quietly wait for the salvation of the LORD.

LAMENTATIONS 3:26

For we are made partakers of Christ, if we hold the beginning of our confidence steadfast unto the end…

HEBREWS 3:14

Wherefore gird up the loins of your mind, be sober, and hope to the end for the grace that is to be brought unto you at the revelation of Jesus Christ.

1 PETER 1:13

And now, Lord, what do I wait for? My hope is in You.

PSALM 39:7 NKJV

8

"I DON'T HAVE TO GO TO CHURCH TO BE A CHRISTIAN"

"Iron rusts from disuse, stagnant water loses its purity and in cold weather becomes frozen; even so does inaction sap the vigors of the mind."
LEONARDO DA VINCI

It's Sunday morning and sister Suzie Rottenheart, a bedtime Baptist, rolls over to hit the remote and join the chapel of the tube. Why should she go to church when she can get it on television and get just as much out of it as a walk in the woods? It is not Christmas or Easter, and her nephew is not starring in a drama this morning, so in bed she will stay. After all, she works for a living and Sunday is supposed to be a day of rest.

MISSING IN ACTION

I can remember seeing John Wayne's last movie, "The Shootist," way back in the late 70s. In it, he explained that the mountains were his church and he did not need to darken the door of a building to worship the Lord.

I can remember something within me thinking "AMEN!" when he said it, too. Now mind you, I also gave him an amen when he said, "I won't be wronged. I won't be insulted. I won't be laid a hand upon. I don't do these things to other people and I require the same from them." Both felt really good and both had nothing to with God.

The latter statement is the reason why he wouldn't go to church. His creed of "I will not be wronged or insulted," would not allow him to be submitted to godly relationships in the first place. I guess his creed of "I won't be laid a hand upon," kept him out of charismatic churches – little joke for us Holy Rollers.

If the question is, can a Christian miss church without missing Heaven, the answer is absolutely, "Yes." But the question brings forward a deceiving answer because other questions still need to be asked. I would be the first in line to say you don't have to go to church to be saved. I would also be in the line that says these things as well:

A Christian cannot be effective or successful long-term without being connected and submitted to other believers.

A Christian will find it extremely difficult to discover their identity, purpose, or destiny apart from the fellowship, encouragement, and teaching of a loving church family.

A Christian will not grow the way he is meant to grow without being connected, committed, and submitted to the church – the Body and Bride of Christ.

A Christian will miss out on the bulk of what God is speaking to him if he is not under the teaching of a Spirit-led pastor.

A Christian will not be able to use his God-given gifts without being a part of a fellowship of believers.

A Christian will miss out on great life-changing moves of God by not being joined with other Christians.

A KINGDOM-PURPOSED MIND SET

When you become a Christian, you are called into a *relationship* with God (1 Corinthians 1:9) and it is a wonderful thing. I John 1:3 also makes it clear we enter a fellowship that goes at least two ways: **with God and with other Christians.** It is the fellowship with Christians that is not always wonderful.

Now, I have good friends who are kingdom-minded Christians and they maintain healthy Christian relationships without going to church very often. I know this can happen, but I also know they are the exceptions to the general rule. These are kingdom -minded people who stay connected and submitted to the Body through their various ministries. Unless that is your case, you ought to get in church.

The New Testament never divides Christians into the church members and the non-church members. All the way through, it assumes everybody participates in his or her local assembly. It gives no examples of Christians who belong to the "universal church," but have no link with a local church.

Any idea of enjoying salvation and being a Christian in isolation is just plain foreign to the New Testament. It is not there. Anytime Christians were within a certain range of each other in the New Testament, they got together and worshipped. In the book of Acts, every time the apostle Paul came to a town where there were no Christians, he won a few converts and immediately organized them into a little church. The next thing he did was ordain and appoint pastors not only to feed and lead those congregations, but to put them in order.

> *For this reason, I left you in Crete, that you should set in order the things that are lacking and appoint elders in every city as I commanded you.*
>
> **TITUS 1:5**

The church must be together to carry out its purposes. This is not a hard thing to understand.

A SIGN OF THE TIMES

There is a carnal part of us that does not want to be joined to the body. In these last days, the Bible is clear that there will be a large group of "separatists" within "Churchianity" – people who become religious in trying not to be religious. It is sad the very people who have this problem usually refuse to admit it is, in fact, their carnal nature that keeps them separate from the church, not the typical excuses they like to hide behind.

The half-brother of Jesus, Jude, spoke of these folks in his incredible book in verse 18 and 19.

How that they told you there should be mockers in the last time, who should walk after their own ungodly lusts. These be they who separate themselves, sensual, having not the Spirit.

When it all comes down to it, the spirit of this generation has become greater in these mavericks than the Spirit of the Lord. The reason so many people, or so-called Christians, do not want to be committed to a group of Christians is simply because they are not kingdom-minded people. They are wrapped up in themselves and their own little worlds. That mindset demands all of their attention.

SPIRITUAL DNA

Just like in our physical bodies, I believe with all my heart that there is something written within the body of Christ – something invisible that says, "This one should be lined up and connected with that one. This one should be fed by that one and helped by another one." Just like physical DNA, I believe in spiritual DNA.

A nose is only a growth if it is not in the right place. Perfect as it might be, it still can never be everything it is supposed to be until it is connected to the correct members of the body. Worse yet, the whole body suffers if that nose is rebellious and will not submit to where it is supposed to be.

If you are not connected and functioning within the body of Christ, not only are you not all you can be, neither are we.

THERE GOES THE NEIGHBORHOOD

This kind of mindset has caused a lot of people to miss out on some of the best things God has had for them simply because they were not there when Jesus showed up.

Some of the best things about God are not taught, they are **caught**. They are imparted and come from the anointing that flows from one life to another. It is one of those things that you "just have to be there" if you're going to be transformed.

Even though thousands should have packed the upper room as Jesus commanded, there were only 120 willing to put up with the other 119 long enough to be there when the Holy Spirit began to baptize them. If you missed that meeting, you just missed it. Period. Sure, there were other opportunities, but if you missed that prayer gathering, you missed a life-changing move of God. The same can be said for the gathering of the church in Acts chapter 4.

And when they had prayed, the place was shaken where they were assembled together; and they were all filled with the Holy Ghost, and they spake the Word of God with boldness.
ACTS 4:31

In Matthew chapter 25, Jesus gave the parable of ten virgins. Do you know what He called the five believers who were not at the house when Jesus showed up? **Foolish!**

It is just plain foolish to be a Christian and not be joined to the body of Christ. We all have our reasons for not being there, but so did the five foolish virgins. I know there are a lot of churches, congregations, and ministries that are not worth the paper their 5013c is written on, but that's no excuse to not be connected somewhere. If this is you, you need to get plugged in today. God has something for you that you're not going to get sitting in your underwear in front of the hell-a-vision. God can break the curse of any addiction, even if it is your butt's addiction to the couch.

GET UP! Find yourself a church that feeds your spirit, inspires your heart, and encourages you to walk closer to the Lord.

BE ALL YOU CAN BE

Here are some irreplaceable pieces of the Christian walk that cannot happen when you live in isolation from the church:

Use of Spiritual Gifts – 1 Corinthians 12 makes it clear God has given spiritual gifts to every Christian. Verse 7 states unmistakably that these abilities are not provided to make you feel good; they are abilities to minister that should be used for the common good! That means your gifts are supposed to be helping the rest of us. 1 Peter 4:10 commands us to use spiritual gifts to help each other. The same passage makes it clear we meet with other Christians so they can use their gifts to strengthen us.

Mutual Ministry – As already discussed, the church is pictured as a body in 1 Corinthians 12. Paul explains each part of the body exists to meet the needs of other parts of that body. In the same way, God intends each of us to meet the needs of other believers using our strengths to help in their areas of weakness. 1 Corinthians 12:21 puts it this way: "The eye cannot say to the hand, 'I have no need of you.' Neither can a Christian say to the other members, 'I have no need of you.'" But lots of members say it every day to their own detriment.

The New Testament is full of "one another" commands. We are to comfort one another (1Thessalonians 4:18), build up one another (1Thessalonians 5:11), confess our sins to one another (James 5: 16), pray for one another (James 5:16), and many more. How can we obey these directives if we stay away from one another?

Accountability – God designed the church to be a place where spiritual leaders could watch out for our welfare as a shepherd guards the sheep (1 Peter 5:1-4; Hebrews 13:17). A Christian who answers only to himself can easily rationalize sinful attitudes or actions. Regular contact with other Christians can keep us sharp and keep us right. I love the verse that says, "Iron sharpens iron," but do you realize that a side effect of that process is that sparks will eventually fly? Don't let that keep you from getting sharpened.

A single verse should be a sufficient answer for the Christian who says he doesn't need to go to church. Hebrews 10:25 warns against "forsaking the assembly of yourselves together, as the manner of some is."

You can stay disconnected if you want to. You can be one of the 96 out of every 100 Americans who choose not to celebrate Jesus and hear the preaching of the Word. But you can't do it without being irrelevant, uninformed, and without missing out on exactly what you need. **There is no way you can be right with God and wrong with His people.** More than that, those of us who are joined together need you with us. It's just not the same without you.

Scripture to invade your soul when thinking, "I don't have to go to church to be a Christian"

Be devoted to one another in brotherly love.
Honor one another above yourselves.

ROMANS 12:10 NIV

Those that be planted in the house of the LORD
shall flourish in the courts of our God.

PSALM 92:13

Just as each of us has one body with many members, and these members do not all have the same function, so in Christ we who are many form one body, and each member belongs to all the others.

ROMANS 12:4-5 NIV

And let us consider one another in order to stir up love and good works, not forsaking the assembling of ourselves together, as is the manner of some, but exhorting one another, and so much the more as you see the day approaching.

HEBREWS 10:24-25 NKJV

9

"GOD WANTS TOO MUCH OUT OF ME"

"Just as our eyes need light in order to see, our minds need ideas in order to conceive."
NAPOLEON HILL

"So, let me get this straight," said the young man across from my desk. "I quit smoking weed. I moved out of my girlfriend's house. I don't have any friends except here at church, and you're telling me God still wants more?"

"Yes."

"How much more, Pastor Troy?"

"Everything. All of it. He's after you, boy, and He's not going to quit."

I've had this same conversation with many people including the good-looking fat man in the mirror from time to time. We all have a selfish part of us that wants to tell God to "talk to the hand" when it comes to asking more out of our life. There are times when we need to know what a right mind is and this is one of those times.

Let's look at what the Word says:

> *I beseech you therefore, brethren, by the mercies of God, that ye present your bodies a living sacrifice, holy, acceptable unto God, which is your reasonable service.*
> **ROMANS 12:1**

What does it mean to present our bodies as a living sacrifice? It means to lay it down and give it up. It doesn't say we are to present "a part" of our body. It says we are supposed to sacrifice and make holy *all* of ourselves – every single part. Brother, as we say here in Texas, that's a tall order.

How tall of an order is it?

According to this scripture, presenting your body as a living sacrifice is neither the 43rd plateau of deep spiritual things, nor is it the secret handshake of the inner sanctum of high spiritual achievement. We think it's an extremely tall order, but in the above verse, the Bible says just the opposite.

It's only your "***reasonable service***." It's the sensible, sufficient, and inexpensive way to serve the Lord.

How can God think it's no big deal for you to give Him all your life? I'll tell you how: He owns it!

LET'S MAKE A DEAL

He doesn't just own part of your life. He owns all of it, and it's not that big of a deal when you turn all of it over to Him. If you lived in my house rent free and I showed up saying I wanted to use my house, I would not consider it a big deal if you handed me the keys. It is my house. It's your privilege to live in my house, but it is still my house. If you want to bargain with me

and just give me two closets and a bathroom, you insult me by giving me only those three tiny parts of my own house. I would tell you, "Hey, this is your reasonable service."

For you were bought with a price; therefore, glorify God in your body and in your spirit, which are God's.
1 CORINTHIANS 6:20 NKJV

What's real is we all bargain with God from time to time. We all do it, but God helps us to have a right mind.

The cure to the thinking pattern of "God wants too much out of me" is a proper assessment of who truly owns your life.

A TRIP IN THE SPIRIT

The Spirit of God showed John what things look like after Jesus returns. John also saw you and I standing there in that day singing a song. Look at the words of the song we will be singing in perfect pitch:

> *"You are worthy to take the scroll, and to open its seals; For You were slain and have redeemed us to God by Your blood out of every tribe and tongue and people and nation. And have made us kings and priests to our God; and we shall reign on the earth."*
>
> **REVELATION 5:9-10 NKJV**

Sooner or later, we all come to the revelation of how God does not ask too much. Is there a price we have to pay? Yes, there is. It is a lifetime of choosing the things of God, rather than what we or anybody else tells us we should want. There is a required commitment on our part to be passionate about our relationship with Christ, and to keep growing and learning. We have to do things we don't want to do and are asked to walk away from things our flesh cries out for. In fact, we are asked to be people we know we are incapable of being. However, the promise of God is that, with God, all things are possible.

More than that, we are asked to keep our mouths shut when we are capable of chewing up our opponent and spitting them out. We are asked to speak up and be counted when we would rather fade into the background like the lobster in the restaurant aquarium. We are asked to be committed to the Body of Christ when we don't feel like giving, getting up, or putting up with sister Suzie Rottenheart.

We want to bargain for the life God has given us – to make a deal. We need to be careful of this mentality because it screams that we are getting ripped off when nothing could be further from the truth.

"If you don't get what you want out of life, it is a sign either that you did not seriously want it, or that you tried to bargain over the price."
RUDYARD KIPLING

SERVING A TYRANT

In 2 Chronicles 12:1-8, we find a king named Rehoboam and an Egyptian tyrant by the name of Shishak. The Bible says Rehoboam "strengthened himself" or, in other words, he prospered and got his act together. When he did, he walked out on God. A lot of people do that. I have seen it over and over again. Some people can only walk with God as long as all hell is breaking loose. People get a cancer report or an IRS hit and they suddenly operate in all nine gifts of the Holy Spirit. But as soon as they get a little strength, it is out of church and back to their own agenda they go. Rehoboam did that and it caught up with him.

Shishak showed up at the gates of Jerusalem. When he did, Rehoboam decided it was time to get right with God again. Because he repented, the Lord had mercy on him, but read very carefully what the Lord had to say:

> *And when the LORD saw that they humbled themselves, the word of the LORD came to Shemaiah (the Prophet) saying, "They have humbled themselves; therefore, I will not destroy them, but I will grant them some deliverance; and My wrath shall not be poured out upon Jerusalem by the hand of Shishak.* Nevertheless, they shall be his servants; that they may know My service, *and the service of the kingdoms of the countries.*
> **2 CHRONICLES 12:7 & 8**

The New Living Translation puts verse 8 this way:

"...so that they can learn how much better it is to serve Me than to serve earthly rulers."

The world-famous Pastor Troy Paraphrase Version (PTPV) puts it this way:

I'm going to let them serve a tyrant for a while so they can know the difference between serving Me and serving a tyrant.

If you gripe and complain that God is too difficult to serve, He might just let you serve something other than Him for a while. The Lord decided He would teach Rehoboam to be happy when he served the Lord. God said it then, and He is still saying it today, "I am not a tyrant, so don't act like I am."

SERVICE WITH A SMILE

God has terrible things on a leash – just like Shishak – that want to invade your life and chew you to pieces. If you refuse to serve God the way He wants you to, He will let go of the terrible things wanting to rule over you.

Tyrants are not just dictators and sharp dressed military men from third world countries. They are also spirits who hold your heart captive. They tell you to be stressed out and full of anxiety. Tyrants are also circumstances that incarcerate all your free time and never allow you to love your family. A tyrant can also be an unbelievable disgrace or embarrassment that will hold your creativity hostage and imprison your goals and dreams.

There are hundreds of thousands of households in America right now that have never served a worldly tyrant, yet the parents are being held hostage and the teenagers are being enslaved by a dictatorial regime of drug abuse or video game addiction.

These are the things that He is holding back from you because you have decided to serve Him. A tyrant – an oppressor – does not always come in human form. There are many abusive overlords that, if God were to let go of His leash, would gladly make you a slave to depression, despair, failure, anger, self-pity, and spiritual bankruptcy.

Do you want God to allow these things to take over your life? No? Stay in His service and stay happy about it. If you leave the reservation, you will walk out from under His protection.

God is looking for service with a smile – for people who are glad they are serving Him instead of drugs. He wants people who are happy to answer to His authority and not the kingdom of hell. Father God wants folks who are cheerful about doing a work for Him, who feel fortunate to be in His Kingdom, and serve with a glad heart. That's not unreasonable.

God doesn't love a giver. God loves a cheerful giver.
2 CORINTHIANS 9:7

How badly do you want to reach your potential and fulfill your true purpose in life? How intent are you about passing down a blessing instead of a curse? How real is your desire to be clean, victorious, and full of the peace of God? Are you hungry for Christ? If so, it will take passionate commitment on your part to keep growing, learning, and moving forward.

You will be required to have a different mentality and an ability to combat your brain when it says, "God wants too much out of me." It is not too much. It is your reasonable service.

SUMMARY PAGE

"God wants too much from me" Spiritual Beef Jerky / Truth for Meditation

1. God will never ask you for anything you do not have within your power to give Him.
2. God never commands you to do anything without giving you the ability to do it.
3. God never asks you to give Him anything that doesn't already belong to Him.
4. The Bible calls the giving up of 100 percent of our bodies as a sacrifice our "reasonable service."
5. The thesaurus lists "reasonable" as sensible, rational, not bad, and inexpensive.
6. The reason it is reasonable for us to hand over our lives to the Lord is because He is the one who has bought and paid for it. In other words, when He asks us for anything, even if it is everything, He is not asking for too much.
7. God is not a tyrant and He doesn't appreciate it when we act like He is. According to 2 Chronicles 12, He will sometimes unleash a tyrant to teach us the difference between serving God and serving something less.
8. God is not looking for your service. God is looking for your service with a smile.
9. God does not need your abilities. God wants you to be happy you are serving Him.

Scripture to invade your soul when you're thinking, "God wants too much from me."

Jesus said to him, "No one who puts his hand to the plow and looks back is fit for the kingdom of God."

LUKE 9:62 RSV

If any man serve me, let him follow me; and where I am, there shall also my servant be: if any man serve me, him will my Father honor.

JOHN 12:26

"Whoever desires to come after Me, let him deny himself, and take up his cross, and follow Me. For whoever desires to save his life will lose it, but whoever loses his life for My sake and the gospel's will save it. For what will it profit a man if he gains the whole world, and loses his own soul? Or what will a man give in exchange for his soul? For whoever is ashamed of Me and My words in this adulterous and sinful generation, of him the Son of Man also will be ashamed when He comes in the glory of His Father with the holy angels.

MARK 8:34-38 NKJV

Do you not know that your body is the temple of the Holy Spirit who is in you, whom you have from God, and you are not your own? For you were bought at a price; therefore, glorify God in your body and in your spirit, which are God's.

1 CORINTHIANS 6:19-20 NKJV

10

"SOMETHING BAD IS GOING TO HAPPEN"

AKA, "DEATH IS AFTER ME"

"Men are not prisoners of fate,
but prisoners of their own minds."
FRANKLIN D. ROOSEVELT

"Rule your mind or it will rule you."
HORACE

"All battles are fought by scared men
who'd rather be someplace else."
JOHN WAYNE, IN HARM'S WAY

Impending doom is a terrible feeling. I get that feeling every time I step onto an airplane. Is doomsday really inevitable? A famous story I remember from elementary school seems to say so.

THE SULTAN AND HIS SERVANT: AN ANCIENT FABLE

The Sultan was residing in his palace when his favorite servant came running in from the garden. He begged his master for the fastest horse from the stable so he could ride to Damascus.

"I was at the market as you sent me," the young man said, "when Death appeared and stalked me. I barely escaped before he spoke to me. Now I must flee to Damascus. Death is after me Master!" The Sultan gave his servant his very best horse.

After an embrace, the servant rode away from the palace with only the clothes on his back.

All night long he rode until his horse collapsed from exhaustion. Leaving the horse behind, he ran from one sand dune to another until he arrived at the gates of Damascus. What was usually a three-day journey had been traveled in only one. He would be safe here.

That same afternoon, the Sultan went down into the market. In the midst of the crowd and unnoticed by others, stood Death with a puzzled look.

The Sultan confronted Death, saying, "How dare you threaten my very best servant? You have disrupted my house and caused him to flee for his life!"

"I didn't mean to threaten him," Death replied. "I was startled to find him here in this market today when I have an appointment with him in Damascus tomorrow."

I read that as a sixth-grader in Joshua Middle School. I learned something that day – something that wasn't true.

THE HEEVIE JEEVIES

Sometimes, for no reason, a good and Godly person can get the feeling something bad is about to happen with an attachment of "there is nothing you can do about it." This theme transcends all cultures throughout all times and beats up on saved and pagan alike. Everybody gets the heevie jeevies now and then. It is a feeling of impending doom and sickening dread that threatens us.

In this generation, teenagers flocked by the millions to a movie called *Final Destination* and the popular sequel that followed it. A modern version of the ancient story of the sultan and his servant, it is a really scary movie about a bunch of friends who cheat death and spend the next two hours trying to run from it. The conclusion is that once death is after you, there is nothing you can do about it. It is going to get you.

I have something to tell you that will turn that 2-hour movie into a five-minute flick. Before I deflate that balloon and set you free, let me tell you about an incredible thing that happened to me when coming back from a mission trip.

A ROOM WITH A VIEW

We had spent a whole week seeing God do incredible things and I was beat. The night before returning home, we were staying at the Heradura Hotel in San Jose, Costa Rica.

My room had a jacuzzi and I was planning on really suffering for Jesus that night. I fired it up, climbed in, and fell asleep within just a few minutes. Instead of peaceful bliss, I was attacked by a spirit of terror that I don't know how to describe. An alarm went off inside my chest and something way past fear descended on me like a blanket.

A nightmare from hell took over my mind and it was an experience I will never forget. Instantly, I was aware I was on a plane and it was going down. The oxygen masks had dropped and everyone on board was crying, praying, or screaming. I was mesmerized by the entire environment

when I noticed the stewardess in front of me make it to her chair – the one that faced the rest of us – and buckle herself in. She was terrified and biting her lower lip. She noticed I was watching her, and we made eye contact.

"This isn't fair," she said blankly. "This is my first flight in three years and now we are all going to die."

As soon as she said it, there was a horrible roar and a climactic boom. I woke up with my face under water. Jumping up, I splashed water all over the bathroom. I climbed out of the tub so scared I was sick. My heart did not slow down for more than an hour. It was awful.

COFFEE, TEA, OR PROZAC

The next morning, I made it to the airport with plenty of time to spare because I didn't sleep after my little "visitation." Now, the San Maria Airport was under construction at the time and a new terminal had been opened just a week earlier. I was one of the first people at gate for Dallas and I still had two hours before boarding. Because of construction, the sign had not been posted yet. An American Airlines stewardess came walking down the hall looking for the gate number with a bag in tow. I knew what she was going to ask before she said anything.

"Is this the gate for American to Dallas?"

"As far as I know," I replied. "It's hard to tell, but that's what all of us here think."

"They are really trying to improve the airport," she said, pointing at all of the construction. Then what she said next sent my heart into my throat. "I haven't been here in a long time. I have been gone for three years and it's my first flight back."

I don't really know what she said next because I didn't hear. I was too busy trying not to have a heart attack. It was as if someone had injected the poison of terror into my veins.

That clinched it. The vision was real. The plane was going to crash and there was nothing I could do about it. I was absolutely 100 percent convinced there was zero probability of survival.

I began to create a plan for missing that flight. I wondered if I should say anything to the people there, explaining that I was a pastor on a mission trip and I had a dream. Maybe that would give me some kind of spiritual credentials. Maybe I would call my friend and ask him to come pick me up, explaining that I didn't feel right about leaving Costa Rica just then. Maybe I could just not get on that plane and catch the next flight.

At that moment, there was only one thing I knew for certain: I was not getting on that airplane. I went over the phone conversation in my head that I would have with Leanna.

"Honey, I'm not getting on that airplane."

"Why not, Troy?"

"Because I think it's going to crash."

"What makes you think it's going to crash?"

"Because last night I had a terrible dream..."

At this point in my mental conversation, a red flag slowly began to wave and the idiot light in my conscience began to flicker. Since when did I base my decisions on a demonic attack? I know what the Word says, and for the life of me, I could not make it line up with my actions.

"The just shall live by dreams."
No, I couldn't find the scripture.

"The just shall live by feelings of terror."
No, I had never read it.

"The just shall live by premonitions."
Nope.

The just shall live by faith.
REPEATED FOUR TIMES IN ROMANS 1:17, GALATIANS 2:20 & 3:11, AND HEBREWS 10:38

Now I was back living in the Word again. The correct juices began to flow. There was no way this thing, powerful as it was, was of God. I thought about the sick, terrible horror I was feeling and wondered aloud, "How many times have I felt like that in the presence of the Lord?" Not once.

This was not a coincidence. It was a spiritual set-up designed to keep me off that plan. I was not being led by peace, so it couldn't be the Holy Spirit. I boarded, still really scared, but confident I was making the right choice. I prayed all the way home. I got on some people's nerves around me, but I know today that plane, with me on it, was the safest plane flying.

NEWS FLASH

This whole "death is after me" thing can be hammered down if you know the Word. When I feel like something bad is going to happen, I can tell the devil "news flash" – there is always going to be something bad that happens until the white throne judgment.

Yet man is born to trouble as surely as sparks fly upward.
JOB 5:7 NIV

David declared that his enemies were always after him. Paul wrote that an evil day is coming in Ephesians chapter 6. It says we need to armor up so we can stand when it gets to us.

Yes, bad things happen. However, that is no reason to be fearful. Yes, trouble is out there, but that's no reason to let your heart jump into your throat and change your agenda.

When "Stonewall" Jackson was asked how he could stand still amidst the bullets and cannonballs at the battle of Bull Run he replied, "The day I will die was chosen before I was born. Why should I fear it? Until that day and on the day, I will trust the Lord."

To hell with the devil who says he is out to get me because I am out to get him! Through Jesus, I have made it my life's mission to steal as many souls from hell – to snatch as many people from his miserable hand as possible. I have a very long track record of being trouble to that cosmic punk and overcoming all he has to throw at me. Why should I fear?

BACK TO THE MOVIES

Do you remember I said I knew how to turn that two-hour horror movie into a five-minute dud? Let me lob a grenade into your feeling of impending doom. There is a great misunderstanding in the story of the *Sultan's Servant* and in the tales of movies like *Final Destination.*

All it takes to correct that feeling that says, "Death is after you and there is nothing you can do about it," is to know the truth and the truth will make you free. Here's the truth:

Death is not after you. Death already has you. Death caught you before you were even born.

Therefore, just as through one man, sin
entered the world, and death through sin,
and thus death spread to all men,
ROMANS 5:12 NKJV

Death isn't out there chasing anybody! It doesn't have to because it already has us all. Death never has and never will pursue you. It doesn't need to. You fearing death is like someone who is scared they might live in Texas, not knowing they already live in Texas. It is just stupid.

THE HOUND ON YOUR TRAIL

You are being chased, but not by death. C.S. Lewis called Jesus "The Hound of Heaven." Jesus is after all of us. He is the God who pursues. He is chasing you down and hot on your trail. Death is not after you. Life is, and life has a name; JESUS!

He has followed you into every mess you've ever made. He has chased you, tracked and trailed you, hoping you would finally surrender and let Him have you. Why don't you let Him catch you and let Him bless you and give you peace? For those who are saved by Christ, doomsday is not inevitable. Our final destination is an eternity of victory with Him.

The next time you get the heevie jeevies, spiritual acid reflux creeps up, and you begin to feel like the grim reaper has picked your number from life's great lotto – when the devil threatens you with impending doom – remind him that he is not the author and finisher of your faith. Jesus is. He does not have the keys to death. Jesus does. In Revelation 1:17-18, John tells us:

And when I saw Him (Jesus), I fell at His feet as dead. And He laid His right hand upon me, saying unto me, "Fear not; I am the first and the last: I am He that liveth, and was dead; and, behold, I am alive for evermore, Amen; *and have the keys of hell and of death.*"

After you remind the devil of that, tell him to take his threats where the sun don't shine. He knows where to back off to. He's been there before. (Matthew 22:13)

SUMMARY PAGE

"Something bad is going to happen" "Death is after me" Spiritual Beef Jerky / Truth for Meditation

1. The idea that death is after you is a lie from the pit of hell. Death is not after you. Death already has you.
2. Death is not after you, life is. Jesus is after you! He is Life. He is the one on your trail.
3. Even if you were going to die tomorrow, God could add to your years. He did it for King Hezekiah by adding fifteen years to his life.

> *Then the word of the LORD came to Isaiah: "Go and tell Hezekiah, 'This is what the LORD, the God of your father David, says: I have heard your prayer and seen your tears; I will add fifteen years to your life.'"*
> **ISAIAH 38:4-5 NIV**

4. The just do not live by bad dreams or premonitions. Do not put too much stock into a freaked out feeling. You can count on the Word of God, for the just shall live by faith.
5. Jesus Christ has slapped death in the face for all of us. Let us never forget who the real boss is.

Scripture to invade your soul when you think, "Something bad is going to happen" or "Death is after me"

Most assuredly, I say to you, the hour is coming, and now is, when the dead will hear the voice of the Son of God; and those who hear will live. For as the Father has life in Himself, so He has granted the Son to have life in Himself, and has given Him authority to execute judgment also, because He is the Son of Man. Do not marvel at this; for the hour is coming in which all who are in the graves will hear His voice and come forth—those who have done good, to the resurrection of life, and those who have done evil, to the resurrection of condemnation.

JOHN 5:25-29 NKJV

Jesus Christ, who has abolished death and brought life and immortality to light through the gospel…

2 TIMOTHY 1:10 NKJV

My enemies would hound me all day, for there are many who fight against me, O Most High. Whenever I am afraid, I will trust in You. In God (I will praise His word), In God I have put my trust; I will not fear. What can flesh do to me?

PSALM 56:2-4 NKJV

I sought the LORD, and He heard me, and delivered me from all my fears. They looked to Him and were radiant, and their faces were not ashamed. This poor man cried out, and the LORD heard him, and saved him out of all his troubles. The angel of the LORD encamps all around those who fear Him and delivers them.

PSALM 34:4-7 NKJV

I would have lost heart, unless I had believed that I would see the goodness of the LORD in the land of the living. Wait on the LORD; Be of good courage, and He shall strengthen your heart; Wait, I say, on the LORD!

PSALM 27:13-14 NKJV

Why are you cast down, O my soul? And why are you disquieted within me? Hope in God, for I shall yet praise Him for the help of His countenance.

PSALM 42:5 NKJV

The righteous will be in everlasting remembrance. He will not be afraid of evil tidings; His heart is steadfast, trusting in the LORD. His heart is established; He will not be afraid, until he sees his desire upon his enemies.

PSALM 112:6-8 NKJV

The name of the LORD is a strong tower; The righteous run to it and are safe.

PROVERBS 18:10 NKJV

Peace I leave with you. My peace I give to you; not as the world gives, do I give to you. Let not your heart be troubled, neither let it be afraid.

JOHN 14:27 NKJV

For ye shall go out with joy, and be led forth with peace...

ISAIAH 55:12

11

"MY KIDS WILL NEVER GET SAVED"

"Good thoughts and actions can never produce bad results, just as bad thoughts and actions can never produce good results"
JAMES ALLEN

"The word impossible is not in my dictionary."
NAPOLEON BONAPARTE

If "my kids will never get saved" is your thinking pattern, you need to memorize Isaiah 44. Check this out:

> *Yet now hear, O Jacob my servant; and Israel, whom I have chosen: Thus saith the LORD that made thee, and formed thee from the womb, which will help thee; Fear not, O Jacob, my servant; and thou, whom I have chosen. For I will pour water upon him that is thirsty, and floods upon the dry ground: I will pour my spirit upon thy seed, and my blessing upon thine offspring: And they shall spring up as among the grass, as willows by the water courses. One shall say, I am the LORD's; and another shall call himself by the name of Jacob; and another shall subscribe with his hand unto the LORD and surname himself by the name of Israel. Thus saith the LORD the King of Israel, and his redeemer the LORD of hosts; I am the first, and I am the last; and beside me there is no God.*
> **ISAIAH 44:1-6**

Let me dismiss the polite protocol and get right to the point. You may have tried everything. You've prayed and prayed, but don't you dare give up on seeing victory in the lives of your kids.

It is the will of God they should be saved.

It is the will of God they should know the truth.

It is the will of God that they should be reconciled unto the Father and their names be written in the Lamb's book of Life. It can happen. It's going to happen because you are in covenant with the Lord your God, and that covenant does not just apply to your house, your job, and your finances. His covenant also applies and extends to your seed – those are your unborn kids – and your offspring – those are your living children.

It is your job to have a right mind when it comes to believing God for victory in your kids' lives. Do not give up. Make it your business to believe God and have hope when others have fallen out. Let me give you some hope concerning your kids.

MARKED FOR LIFE

About 600 years before Jesus arrived on the scene, there lived an inconspicuous young man, the son of the high priest of Israel. Like most PKs, he had plans for his life other than the ministry. God showed up and changed those plans in a very big way.

His daddy was famous in his generation, but young Jeremiah would become one of the most famous preachers who ever lived. The "weeping prophet," Jeremiah's ministry would be so powerful, we still read his writings more than 2,600 years after he took his first breath of heaven's sweet air.

The reason I bring him up is because at the very beginning of his book, he records something you just have to see.

> *Then the word of the LORD came unto me, saying, "Before I formed thee in the belly I knew thee; and*

> *before thou camest forth out of the womb I sanctified thee, and I ordained thee a prophet unto the nations."*
> **JEREMIAH 1:4&5**

God introduces Himself to this young man and makes him an offer he can't refuse. God essentially says, "Don't you try to tell me who you are not. Let me tell you who you are!" Then God points out three stages of bringing the promise of His salvation and ministry to pass. Let me harp on the first two.

1. **"Before I formed thee in the belly I knew thee..."**

That means before there was ever a plan on earth for the making of Jeremiah, there was a plan in Heaven for that boy. Not only was there a plan, but there was also an identity. He was chosen to be Jeremiah. Before two microscopic cells ever collided to form the first Jeremiah cell, God said, "I knew you." He was on God's heart, in God's incredible mind, and God took his formation very personally.

"I knew you, Jeremiah. I have always known who you are, so let Me tell you who you are."

I pray you and I will let the Lord identify us, not those around us. Certainly, we will not let our past identify us.

Know this, God knows **your** child. He sees your kid every moment of every hour. In Genesis 16:13, God is called El-Roi, "the strong God that sees."

2. **...and before thou camest forth out of the womb I sanctified thee...**

While that one cell divided and multiplied, more than tissue and bone began to appear. Inside the depths of his mother's womb, while his little hands and feet were taking shape, long before anyone would gaze in wonder at a blurry image of a sonogram, God Almighty saw that baby boy and sanctified him.

To sanctify means He marked him. Jeremiah would have something on and within him from the very finger of God Himself that would set him apart from the rest of the world. He was marked for holiness! He wouldn't be able to interpret it at first, but any time he was not walking the walk, he would feel it. When he would run with the crowd and go where the dogs bark, he would always feel off kilter. Something he could not quite put his finger on would yearn for something different, something holy, and something right with God.

Moses had that mark. He woke up one day and, in spite of living with the devil himself, it occurred to him that he had been on the wrong team all his life. For no reason other than the mark of God, he decided his identity was not with Egypt. In fact, it was with God's people.

I remember when that happened to me. The same thing happened to you. If you are a Christian, I do not have to know you to know that a realization came upon you one day. It told you that you had been running with the wrong crowd.

While you were in the world getting high, getting drunk, or getting whatever, there was something within you that said, "You are not marked for this."

You can trust God that while your child was being formed, He marked your baby so that, sooner or later, one way or another, Jesus was going to win that precious life!

BIGGER AND BETTER THAN YOU

Here is another reason to have great hope for your kids and grandkids.

A good friend of mine, Pastor Jim Maxwell, preached a sermon called "The Other Side of the Mountain" and in it, he gave an amazing account of a blessing that comes from the heart of King David. The blessing in him outlived him and went to his kids.

Fifty-six years after David made a special covenant with God, in 1 Kings chapter 11, the Bible says David's son Solomon, who was now king, had turned from the Lord. This was the man whom God had given everything to. He had turned away and God was upset.

In verse 12, He tells him, "I ought to kill you and devastate your kingdom, but I will not because of your daddy, David."

Twenty-seven years after that, Solomon's grandson, Abijah, had turned from the Lord and provoked God to wipe him out. Destruction was everywhere around this man and God spoke to him in 1 Kings chapter 15. He said, "I should kill you. I should let the devil have you. I should let all the plans of your enemies come to pass, but I will not because of your granddad, David."

I believe God will do the same for you if you will remain in covenant with Him. He will keep His promise to all your generations, just like He did with David's bloodline.

Over 300 years after the death of David (2 Kings 19), the Assyrian tyrant Rabshakeh attacked Jerusalem. He surrounded its walls and declared that everybody was going to die. King Hezekiah called for Isaiah the prophet and God spoke to Hezekiah and said, "I will deliver you, but not because of you. It is because of my servant David."

God sent an angel and that one angel killed 185,000 Assyrian soldiers, destroying the Assyrian army in a heartbeat.

AN ANGEL WITH AN ATTITUDE

I have to stop here for a second. Can I just tell you, without making you mad, that angels are not little fat white babies with wings? Angels are warriors and they are chomping at the bit to kill somebody!

When Peter went to defend Jesus with a sword, Jesus told him, "I don't need you to defend me. I have twelve legions of angels at my disposal any time I call for them."

Let's look at that. There are 6,000 soldiers in a legion. Twelve legions are 72,000 soldiers. If one angel could destroy 185,000 men, what could 72,000 angels do? If you do that math, it works out to be over 13 billion people. It's interesting to note that the population of the entire world at the time of Christ was less than 250 million people. The population of the world did not even reach one billion people until 1804! That's amazing to me. There are more people in the USA right now than there were in the entire world at the time of Jesus.

The point is, if twelve legions of angels could take out a minimum of 13 billion people, Jesus held the safety of the entire world in His hands at that moment. He still does.

YOUR KIDS AND YOUR COVENANT

David's blessing went past his life, and again, so does yours. Some of you reading this should be dead, in prison, or at the very least, dying of some addiction or sexually transmitted disease. You should be miserable, without hope, without peace, and without rest. But you read these words with Christ in your life and the Holy Ghost leaping within you because you had a mama, daddy, or a great, great, great, great, somebody that loved the Lord – and that blessing has been passed down to you and me!

Oh, my God, there is hope in that! Have a right mind about God's promise to you. Your kids are coming home. If God can save you, He can save anybody.

SUMMARY PAGE

"My kids will never get saved"
Spiritual Beef Jerky / Truth for Meditation

1. It is the will of God that your kids should be saved.
2. It is the will of God that they should know the truth.
3. It is the will of God that your kids should be reconciled unto the Father and their names written in the Lamb's Book of Life.
4. God knows how to reach them. He knows what it will take.
5. Your covenant with God is extended to your kids.
6. You can trust God to reach your children.
7. The blessing that is in you is bigger than you.
8. If God can save you, He can save anybody.

Scriptures to invade your soul when thinking, "My kids will never get saved."

The children of His servants will inherit it, and those who love His name will dwell there.

PSALM 69:36

The children of Your servants will continue, and their descendants will be established before You.

PSALM 102:28

For I will pour water on him who is thirsty, and floods on the dry ground; I will pour My Spirit on your descendants, and My blessing on your offspring; They will spring up among the grass like willows by the watercourses. One will say, 'I am the LORD's; Another will call himself by the name of Jacob; Another will write with his hand, 'The LORD's, and name himself by the name of Israel.

ISAIAH 44:3-5

And their seed shall be known among the Gentiles,
and their offspring among the people: all that
see them shall acknowledge them, that they are
the seed which the LORD hath blessed.

ISAIAH 61:9

Then Peter said unto them, Repent, and be baptized
every one of you in the name of Jesus Christ for
the remission of sins, and ye shall receive the gift
of the Holy Ghost. For the promise is unto you,
and to your children, and to all that are afar off,
even as many as the Lord our God shall call.

ACTS 2:38-39

But let all those that put their trust in thee rejoice: let
them ever shout for joy, because thou defendest them:
let them also that love thy name be joyful in thee.

PSALM 5:11

"The immature mind hops from one thing to
another; the mature mind seeks to follow through."

HARRY A OVERSTREET

"Pray without ceasing."

1 THESSALONIANS 5:17

12

"IT IS MY WAY OR THE HIGHWAY!"

Pride only breeds quarrels, but wisdom is found in those who take advice.
PROVERBS 13:10 NIV

Jeff Sherrill, of One More International, is the kind of guy who gets things done. He organizes crusades, pastor's conferences, and mission trips for people and churches wanting to make a difference in Central America. He does not know it, but the Lord really used him to show me something that would forever change my life.

Jeff took my good friends Danny MacBrayer, Nick Smades and me to the northern point of Costa Rica to a little village called Los Chiles. Just a few feet south of Nicaragua, it was an excellent place for a lot of pastors to gather.

Most of the time when Jeff puts something together, there are literally hundreds of pastors in attendance and the meetings may last for days. This was what we were expecting. However, when we got there, we found four pastors and about thirty local church members waiting for a good word. It was fine with me, as it would have been with Jeff, except for the fact that a lot of money and planning had gone into this. I could tell right off the bat that Jeff was very disappointed with the person he had placed in charge of the event. Some of the people Jeff was working with were new contacts and they had not done what they said they would.

After he made some inquiries, he came to us. That is when I really saw Jesus in him. He said, "Boys, this looks like it is going to be it. Some of the folks I had trusted to handle this event were new to me and they didn't follow through. I will make different arrangements in the future, but there is nothing we can do about that now."

He pointed back toward the little church as we were standing outside and continued, "I'm sorry it is not what I told you it was going to be, but it is still a good opportunity to really bless the few pastors who are here. So, let's get in there and do our thing." Then Jeff looked at me, smiled and said, **"Blessed are the flexible."**

We went in and preached for a couple of days like there were 1,000 pastors to feed. It turned out to be a really good bunch of services that made a big difference. But the greatest difference made on any pastor was me. "Blessed are the flexible" echoed in my mind throughout the whole trip.

I thought to myself, "Am I a very flexible person?"

Would I have handled that situation differently?

In how many situations can I not be blessed, or even be a blessing, because of my famous inflexibility?

The conclusions I came to all suggested I needed a serious soul invasion. I began to meditate on the good and bad points of being flexible. This is a list of some of those initial thoughts I wrote in my journal:

PROS & CONS

Pro: I can have peace in any situation.
Con: I give up control of that situation.

Pro: I remain an effective witness even though a situation didn't go the way I had planned it.
Con: If I don't throw a fit, it might appear this is the way I thought it should go. In other words, I might look bad.

Pro: I keep a good relationship with Godly people who do things the way I would like them to.

Con: I don't get to chew somebody out and verbally slap them around.

Pro: I remain in the presence of the Holy Spirit and don't run Him off through my "corrupt communication."
Con: My feelings are not expressed and known to everyone there. Yes, this is the one that made me a little bit ill when I saw it in print.

Maybe you have seen this scripture several times, but I happened to come across it while thinking on all of this that night.

> *Let no corrupt communication proceed out of your mouth, but that which is good to the use of edifying, that it may minister grace unto the hearers. And grieve not the Holy Spirit of God, whereby ye are sealed unto the day of redemption. Let all bitterness, and wrath, and anger, and clamour, and evil speaking, be put away from you, with all malice: And be ye kind one to another, tenderhearted, forgiving one another, even as God for Christ's sake hath forgiven you.*
> **EPHESIANS 4:29-32**

All of the pros were about the will of God while all of the cons were about my sinful flesh. After looking at it this way, there was no way that I could not begin to have a "blessed are the flexible" approach to my ministry. I also needed to let it bleed over into all of my life.

I am not saying that I have completely arrived. I still tend to get upset when I work really hard to make something happen and it does not come together the way I would like. I can happily report however, that God has moved me quantum leaps forward in how I react to that disappointment, particularly when it comes to the incompetence of others.

A RIGHT WAY TO DO THINGS

Like most leaders, movers, and shakers, I get a God-given vision and I want it done right. There is nothing wrong with that. I cannot stand it when something is half-way done, especially when the body of Christ half-way does things.

The thing the Lord made real to me is this; just as there is a right way to do all the things that need to be done, **there is a right way to handle those things that do not get done right**. There is a right way to handle yourself in situations that are far less than perfect. There is a right way to conduct yourself when dealing with the ineffectiveness of what you have planned or the incompetence of someone you have trusted to do a job for you.

When it comes to making things happen, you plan, plan, and plan again. Work, work, and work some more, but if after doing all you can do, the thing you want to happen seems like a dud, go with what you have and be the greatest example of Jesus you can possibly be. Make whatever situation you have been handed glorify the Lord. Say

"**Blessed are the flexible**" and retain your witness. Trust the Holy Spirit and let Him lead you through that uncharted territory. There will be a time for corrections after the situation is over, but at that critical point, Jesus is trusting you to make the most out of that mess. Blessed are the flexible.

SPECIAL ORDERS DON'T UPSET US

It doesn't have to be perfect. It just has to be submitted to the will of God. It doesn't always have to be your way. It has to be God's way.

On another trip to Central America, I got off the plane and got through customs faster than usual, only to find out my ride was not there. Though I didn't know it, a storm in the mountains had put my friend way behind schedule. For about an hour and a half, I sat on the curb looking down the street. "Blessed are the flexible."

That was not the time to get upset. I had made every arrangement possible. I had done all I could do. The man I was expecting to pick me up was, and still is, one of the most competent humans I have ever had the privilege of knowing. I double checked my e-mails and saw we had correctly communicated, so having the peace of the Lord, I sat there without any other plans. If they did not show up after a few hours, I would take a cab to a hotel and crash for the night. Maybe I would fly back home the next day or even pray about setting some things up while I was down there. The bottom line was that I had done everything I could do, so blessed are the flexible.

I wonder how many uncomfortable situations you could have real peace in if you would adopt this principle of thinking.

Have you ever considered the fact that Jesus did not have to have everything His way? In fact, He didn't have to have anything His way. He was all about the Father's will for His life.

And He said, "Abba, Father, all things are possible for You. Take this cup away from Me; nevertheless, not what I will, but what You will."
MARK 14:36 NKJV

I want to encourage you to not let yourself lose your mind when things do not go the way you would like them to. Let the Word of God deal with you concerning how you deal with the disappointments of life. Seriously pray about this one issue and ask God to give you an anointing for mercy in stressful situations, because until your flesh assumes room temperature, you are going to have plenty to deal with. Don't just hang in there. You are vulnerable when you hang anywhere. Stand! Make a clear and definitive stand in your thinking that you will have a mind that glorifies and belongs to the Lord in every way.

Scripture to invade your Soul when thinking, "It's my way or the highway."

Not that I speak in regard to need, for I have learned in whatever state I am, to be content: I know how to be abased, and I know how to abound. Everywhere and in all things, I have learned both to be full and to be hungry, both to abound and to suffer need. I can do all things through Christ who strengthens me.
PHILIPPIANS 4:11-13 NKJV

Useless information concerning your brain:

Doctors say that the human brain is a mass of pinkish-gray tissue containing a neural network involving approximately 10 billion nerve cells called neurons. Weighing in at a mere three pounds, the brain operates as the central control system for movement, sleep, hunger, and thirst of all human beings. It controls nearly every vital activity necessary for survival. Furthermore, the brain receives and interprets the multitude of signals being sent by other parts of the body and the outside environment. There are three major divisions of the brain: the forebrain, midbrain, and hindbrain.

Important information concerning your brain:

Your brain has teeth. If you do not command, restrain, and control it, it will chew your life to pieces. You can forget about fighting the devil or overcoming the world until you get real about dealing with what is between your two ears. It is time for you, as a Christian, to take back your God-given mental turf with clear Word-based strategies.

What you need is a ***Soul Invasion.***

Section Two: HEAD GAMES

STRATEGICALLY WINNING THE BATTLE BETWEEN YOUR EARS

"A girl with brains ought to do something with them besides think."
GENTLEMEN PREFER BLONDES

"You can't control your feelings, but you can control your thoughts. It is your thoughts that control your feelings!"
SCOTTY MCKAY

Things You Can Do to Have a Right Mind

Chapter 13: Armor Up

Chapter 14: Climb the Higher Rock

Chapter 15: How to deal with your haters

Chapter 16: Give God your Mouth

Chapter 17: Let's Get Small

Chapter 18: Brain freeze

Chapter 19: Make a List

13

ARMOR UP!

YOUR MENTAL DEFENSE

There should be a lot more going on between your two ears than random thoughts and memories. There should be a strategic plan of action that says, "There are some ways I can think that will cause me to prosper."

Let's look at one here in this chapter on your mental defenses.

YOU GOTTA BE READY!

Nestled between Germany and France, and thrown across the Alps, lies the tiny country of Switzerland. Politically known for its military neutrality, Switzerland is thought by most to be a haven for political correctness and socialist laws. Just the opposite is the reality. Every adult male is issued a military stock assault rifle and a bunch of ammunition by the government and is employed by the militia. Shooting ranges dot the countryside and, because of that, some of the best marksmen in the world come from Switzerland.

Every home in the national of Switzerland has at least one assault rifle and a whole closet of ammo provided by the government.

So, what's my point?

Switzerland is a nation that loves peace, yet its people are armed to the teeth. That nation exists in a constant state of readiness because it understands the following principle:

The nation that experiences the most peace is the nation most prepared for war!

It's the same with you. If you really want peace in your mind, you need to be somebody who is mentally and spiritually armed to the teeth. You have to accept the fact that war is inevitable. You have to refuse to allow yourself to be mesmerized into the belief that you are immune to the ravages of war by the left-wing dummies of this world!

The enemy will take an unprepared Christian into a headlock and slam him into demonically controlled thinking patterns the way Hulk Hogan slams people in the turnbuckle. A Christian who is not at a constant state of readiness is one that makes an easy target for the enemy. So, here's the deal, Sparky:

It is inevitable you will be spiritually attacked in the area of your mind at some point this very day.

Are you ready for that attack? What will you think on when it strikes you? How will you keep the devil from taking over your head? How will you keep him from putting you in a headlock? You better be armored up! You better be ready.

Wherefore take unto you the whole armor of God, that ye may be able to withstand in the evil day, and having done all, to stand.
EPHESIANS 6:13

The evil day is coming my friend. You've got to have your defenses up *before* you get attacked, or you will not be able to stand!

God has not called you to "hang in there." Like I said before, you are vulnerable when you are hanging from something. He has called you to **STAND**. It does no good to stand if you're not armored up, so let's look at how that works.

GET YOUR ACT TOGETHER

There is a great scene in a famous Clint Eastwood movie. The bad guy walks right into a bar where a posse is being put together to chase him down. Stunned, everyone gets quiet and he groans out a simple question.

"Who owns this place?"

From behind the bar, a man by the name of Skinny says he bought it from a man named Greeley for $1,000 dollars. With that, the bad guy pulls the trigger on his shotgun and shoots Skinny dead on the floor.

The sheriff, outraged at what had just happened said,

"Sir, you just killed an unarmed man!"

Just as matter-of-fact as he could, Clint Eastwood replied,

"Well, he should have armed himself."

That is exactly the devil's attitude. If you refuse to arm yourself, the devil will be more than happy to lay you out on the floor. You can cry foul all you want, but it is your job to spiritually take up arms. Otherwise, you just stand there and let the devil have you. Not me! If the devil wants me, he'd better bring a bigger gun because he's not just walking into my head, asking who owns the place, then laying me out because I wouldn't arm myself.

We need to be serious about our spiritual battle. We need to arm ourselves. I want to help wake you up out of your spiritual coma the way that Paul Revere woke up the Militia on April 15, 1776.

Arm yourself because an attack is coming!

A READY MIND

Remember how I said Switzerland was in a constant state of readiness? That's how we need to be. One sign of a mature church and a mature Christian is they make themselves ready. They are prepared. The church Jesus comes back for is described in Revelation 19:7 as a bride that has "made herself ready."

It's not just anything that needs to be ready. Peter made it clear when he said our minds need to be ready.

Feed the flock of God which is among you, taking the oversight thereof, not by constraint, but willingly; not for filthy lucre, but of a ready mind...
1 PETER 5:2

To have a ready mind means to be eagerly prepared to serve. In fact, some translations spell out the end of this verse as "...but to eagerly serve."

The first step to making your mind ready for battle is to grab hold of a willingness to serve God in your thinking.

Who will master your mind? You can't have two masters.

Do you really believe that Jesus Christ wants to rule your mind? If so, you need to be willing to serve Him in your mind.

Are your prepared to let some thoughts go and let some thoughts in?

Are you prepared to think about how much God loves you instead of that one dummy who doesn't?

Are you eager to remember what God has done *for* you instead of what people have done *to* you?

Are you ready to let God give you His plans and goals for your life instead of just thinking about what you want all the time?

If you answered no to any of those questions, then armor up. Repent and get with this program, because these are the places you can stand when that attack come. Believe me when I tell you, it's coming big-time!

You make your mind ready by having an eagerness to mentally serve the Lord. Here are some questions that might help you see how well armored you are:

How are you actively serving the Lord in your mind right now? Do you have honest and realistic mental boundaries? Are there things you will and will not think about? Do you have times of meditation on God's Word? Do you want God to be able to do great things in your mind?

Some people don't. I want God to do great things in my thinking, the same way I want Him to do great things in the jungles of Africa and Central America. I have been on riverboats in Costa Rica and seen God do great things in little villages out in the middle of nowhere. Just like that, I want to see God move in the deep places of my thinking and the dark places of my accepted wisdom. It's just as great a missionary journey and into just as harsh and ruthless an environment.

Have you allowed the Holy Spirit to personally deal with you concerning your mind? Have you let the Lord show you problem and potential problem areas in your thinking? Do you allow the Holy Spirit to convict you in your thinking or is your mind an area you see as off limits to God?

What specific scriptures and Biblical principles do you think on when turning from your mental problem areas? When I feel rejected, I think on Hebrews 13:5 – "I will never leave thee, nor forsake thee." When I am sad that people I hoped would be proud of me are not interested in what I am doing or where I am going, I think on Psalms 41:11– "By this I know that thou favourest me, because mine enemy doth not triumph over me." Do you have a list like that? You should.

KEVLAR COATING YOUR GRAY MATTER

Let's take a look at the armor God gives us:

> *Wherefore take unto you the whole armor of God, that ye may be able to withstand in the evil day, and having done all, to stand. Stand therefore, having your loins girt about with truth, and having on the breastplate of righteousness; and your feet shod with the preparation of the gospel of peace; above all, taking the shield of faith, wherewith ye shall be able to quench all the fiery darts*

of the wicked. And take the helmet of salvation, and the sword of the Spirit, which is the word of God...

EPHESIANS 6:13-17

"A British soldier illustrates the importance of proper headgear"

If you have been saved for very long, you have no doubt already studied this text of scripture. Pay close attention to the very first piece of armor God instructs us to put on.

THE BELT OF TRUTH

The reason TRUTH is seen as a belt here in scripture is because TRUTH is what holds all of your armor together under pressure. Truth has to do with your mind and if you're going to armor up, God says this is the first area you armor up in.

"We must combine the toughness of the serpent with the softness of the dove, a tough mind and a tender heart."

DR. MARTIN LUTHER KING

Another thing you might take note of is this: we are to have our loins girt about with TRUTH. Do you know that your mind is reproductive? Do you realize that you are producing things all the time from the arena of your mind? You protect that part of your life with truth. Not with FACT. With TRUTH.

Truth always supercedes fact. Facts are temporary, carnal, and subject to the perspective of the beholder, but TRUTH is eternal and never changes.

It might be a fact that your husband has left you, but the TRUTH is you are not alone. (Deut. 4:31)

It may be a fact that those around you don't have a clue about what's going on in your life, but the TRUTH is that God knows. (Psalms 1:6)

It may be a fact that there is no physical way to realize your God-given dreams, but the TRUTH is, with God, all things are possible. (Philippians. 4:13)

Fox News Network gives you the facts. The doctor gives you the facts, but it is the Holy Spirit who gives you the truth.

> *Howbeit when He, the Spirit of truth, is come, He will guide you into all truth: for He shall not speak of Himself; but whatsoever He shall hear, that shall He speak: and He will show you things to come.*
> **JOHN 16:13**

If we do not maintain truth in the middle of our mess, we will produce something in that situation not born of God – something illegitimate. God help us to keep ourselves covered!

It is the belt of TRUTH that holds our protective armor together under the pressures we face. That's why God told us to put it on first.

ARMOR AGAINST HEAD BLOWS

The United States has put millions of dollars into the development of the modern military helmet. It's an amazing piece of armor that soldiers cannot do without. It only weighs three pounds and costs 90 dollars, but it's worth its weight in gold to those in the fight.

I saw on Fox News that right after the war in Iraq started, a British solider took several direct hits in his Kevlar helmet while it was on his head, mind you. (See page 131) Look at the picture and see the importance of proper headgear. Now, that's one tough helmet!

In the armor division at Fort Stewart, there is a display case in the battalion headquarters. There are lots of artifacts from Desert Storm and one of the most interesting is a Kevlar helmet. It had been worn by a young private who wouldn't be here except for that helmet. The Kevlar bears the scars of a 7.62, AK-47 bullet. It took a direct hit and the young man lived to tell about it. Had he not been properly dressed for battle at that exact moment, he would have been taken out. It's the same way with you.

Let me tell you why spiritually you've got to have a tough helmet.

Because a blow to the head disorients you. A blow to the head causes you to be confused.

If you're going to fight spiritual battles, you've got to keep your head on straight and the armor the Lord has given is described as a helmet of salvation.

Every battle you fight should be on the turf of being saved. Every battle you fight should be with a perspective of who you are in Christ and who Jesus has called you to be.

The devil will try to disorient you by telling you that you are who people have always said you are. That's a head blow.

The devil will try to confuse you with the recollection of past failures and bad choices. That's a HEAD BLOW.

The devil will try to overwhelm you with the memory of terrible things that have happened to you. That's a HEAD BLOW.

If you fight the devil on these three turfs, you will lose every single time. But the armor that God has given us is a perspective of salvation. Put it on!

When the devil says, "I know the real you. I know how you really are," you put your helmet on and say, "I am saved. That makes me the righteousness of God in Christ."

When the devil comes to you and says, "I know what you've done in the past." Put your helmet on and deflect his attack by saying, "I am a new creature in Christ and behold all things are brand new."

When the devil comes to you and reminds you of all the terrible things that have happened to you, put your helmet on and tell him, "Devil, what you meant for evil, the Lord meant for good. I'm saved, and my life is going to get better and better and better."

Put your helmet on and fight every battle on the turf of Christ Jesus is within you and you will win every time.

Get your armor on and your defenses up. Don't let the devil have your mind. It doesn't belong to him. You are protecting the property of the King.

SUMMARY PAGE

Armor Up!
Spiritual Beef Jerky / Truth for Meditation

1. Mental warfare in inevitable, so I need to be ready for it.
2. If I want to maintain peace in my mind, I have to be mentally armed to the teeth.
3. A Biblical "ready mind" is a mind ready to serve God.
4. The first piece of spiritual armor God commands we put on is the Belt of Truth.
5. Truth is the belt that holds everything together under pressure.
6. We keep the "loins" of our mind covered with the Belt of Truth because spiritually, our minds are reproductive and most of our mind should never be seen.
7. We should live by truth, not by fact. The facts change from day to day, but the truth is eternal.
8. Wearing my helmet of salvation in combat means fighting from an understanding that I am saved.
9. I need to spiritually defend my mind, because it is the property of the Lord.

Scriptures to Invade Your Soul:

Wherefore take unto you the whole armor of God, that ye may be able to withstand in the evil day, and having done all, to stand. Stand therefore, having your loins girt about with truth, and having on the breastplate of righteousness; and your feet shod with the preparation of the gospel of peace; above all, taking the shield of faith, wherewith ye shall be able to quench all the fiery darts of the wicked. And take the helmet of salvation, and the sword of the Spirit, which is the word of God:

EPHESIANS 6:13-17

Feed the flock of God which is among you, taking the oversight thereof, not by constraint, but willingly; not for filthy lucre, but of a ready mind;

1 PETER 5:2

Who gave Himself for us, that He might redeem us from all iniquity, and purify unto Himself a peculiar people, zealous of good works.

TITUS 2:14

14

CLIMB THE HIGHER ROCK

A PLACE OF STRATEGIC ADVANTAGE

Prayer puts you in touch with the infinite
and prepares your mind for the finite.
PETER DANIEL

He maketh my feet like hinds' (deer's) feet:
and setteth me upon my high places.
2 SAMUEL 22:34

You wouldn't think it, but Texas has more square miles of coastline than any other state. We have a desert in the west, the big thicket in the east, the hill country in the center of the state, the valley in the south, the Palo Duro Canyon, vast grasslands, great plains, and the murky swamps and wetlands of the southeast.

I love Texas; it's got it all. I used to think Texas had everything but mountains until I made my first trip down to the Big Bend. Believe it or not, Texas has mountains, and not just little mountains either. They are really big mountains by anyone's standard and well worth the drive to see them.

Even though I'm a flatlander from Johnson County, I love mountains and I love to visit them. I am amazed at how big some of them are.

The elevation at the top of Pike's Peak is 14,110
Mount Rainier in Washington State: 14,410

Mount McKinley in Alaska: 20,320
K2 in Kashmir: 28,250
Mount Everest on the Nepal-Tibet border: 29,028

When Sir Edmund Hillary reached the summit of Mt. Everest on May 29, 1953, he was asked why he had attempted such an incredible challenge. His answer; "Because it was there."

God loves the mountains as well. There are some high places in the Lord that few people are up to the challenge of climbing. God Himself is called the "Most High" God.

These places I am talking about are reserved for a very elite few. People who are willing to get up off the couch and be the people He has called them to be. These places are above the muck and the mire. Above the filth and the noise of our everyday lives. Places where the air is clean, and things make sense on a greater scale.

All of us, as people of God, need to find these places in Christ. We all have a God-given, spiritual ability to get up there too.

He maketh my feet like hinds' (deer's) feet:
and setteth me upon my high places.
2 SAMUEL 22:34

There is no neutral in your spiritual gearbox. You are either climbing higher, reaching toward the things of God or you are sinking into the muck and mire of your flesh and your world.

THE END OF YOUR ROPE

Hear my cry, O God; attend unto my prayer. From the end of the earth will I cry unto thee, when my heart is overwhelmed: lead me to the rock that is higher than I.
PSALM 61:1-2

On Thanksgiving morning of 2000, my wife and I were staying in a crummy hotel in London, England. It was our very first mission trip there and that day was going to be a biggie.

I had woken up very early because my internal clock was out of whack. When I opened my Bible, my eyes fell on Psalms 61. God really moved that morning.

When David says that he will cry out to God from the ends of the world, he is not talking about a geographical location. In modern terms, we would translate that phrase as ***the end of his rope***. To stress the point, the very next thing he says is that his heart is overwhelmed. He really is at the end of his rope or at his wits end.

One-thousand years later, one of the last things Jesus said before His ascension into heaven is that He would "be with us always, even unto the ends of the world." He was saying He would be with us at the end of our rope – when our hearts are overwhelmed.

You and I need to learn how to find the presence of Jesus when our hearts are overwhelmed. Our ability to find the presence of Jesus at the end of our rope is determined by our ability to seek Jesus at the end of our rope. Oh, how much easier it is to throw a fit than bow a knee!

A VIEW FROM ABOVE

You probably are very aware of the time Jesus asked His disciples what the word on the street was about Him. Read it very carefully and let God show you something new.

When Jesus came into the coasts of Caesarea Philippi, He asked His disciples, saying, "Whom do men say that I the Son of man am?" And they said, "Some say that thou art John the Baptist; some, Elias; and others, Jeremiah, or one of the prophets." He saith unto them, "But whom say ye that I am?" And Simon Peter answered and said, "Thou art the Christ, the Son of the living God." And Jesus answered and said unto him, Blessed art thou, Simon Barjona; for flesh and blood hath not revealed it unto thee, but my Father which is in heaven. And I say also unto thee, that thou art Peter, and upon this rock I will build my church; and the gates of hell shall not prevail against it. And I will give unto thee the keys of the kingdom of heaven; and whatsoever thou shalt bind on earth shall be bound in heaven, and whatsoever thou shalt loose on earth shall be loosed in heaven.

MATTHEW 16:13-19

Most people have falsely speculated that Jesus is saying Peter is the rock the church will be built on. That is not the case. Peter has stepped onto the rock the church would be built on. THE ROCK JESUS IS TALKING ABOUT IS REVELATION KNOWLEDGE – the ability to know something straight from the Father. Jesus Christ is revealed by revelation knowledge and this spiritual download is essential to every human being who calls himself or herself a Christian.

Revelation knowledge is knowing or seeing something the way God knows or sees something. This is fundamental Christianity. This is the rock where the church starts. This is a view from above.

The next time your heart is overwhelmed, and your mind is freaked out – the next time you are at the "end of your world" as both King David and King Jesus have put it – allow the Lord to lead you to a higher rock. Let God show you your situation the way He sees it. Consent to the leading of the Holy Spirit concerning your understanding of whatever is causing your anxiety. Say, "Lord, lead me to the rock that is higher than I." In other words, "Show me how to see this the way you see it. Show me how to know this the way you do."

Submit your mind to the mind of Christ.

When you get a real download of revelation knowledge and you see your situation from God's point of view, it is like climbing up to a higher place where the air is clean and things make sense. That's a higher rock worth climbing.

SUMMARY PAGE

Climb the Higher Rock
Spiritual Beef Jerky/ Truth for Meditation

1. According to 2 Samuel 22:34, we Christians possess a God-given ability to climb out of whatever mental mess we find ourselves in.
2. When David says in Psalms 61 that he will "cry out to God from the ends of the world," we translate that in our day as "from the end of his rope."
3. Our ability to find God at our wits end is based upon our ability to seek God at our wits end.
4. Jesus has built the entire church on the rock of revelation knowledge. Therefore, all have access to a supernatural download from the mind of Christ to our mind. If we can see things the way God sees them, we will not be overwhelmed.
5. You should ask the Lord right now to give you His mind concerning whatever is overwhelming you. Submitting your mind to Christ is the key to having true mental victory in your life.
6. God knows how to lead you into right thinking concerning your mess – past, present or future. He wants to turn your mess into a message that will help and heal you.

15

HOW TO HANDLE YOUR HATERS

The more you use your brain, the more brain you will have to use.
GEORGE A. DORSEY

Do you have people who hate you, talk bad about you and want to see you fail? Are you dealing with somebody or some group that is jealous or envious of you? I hope so. Because there is no way you can be a part of the body of Christ without having someone persecute you. There is no way you can have anything in your life worth having without someone else being mad at you for having it. This is the world we live in and you need to know how to successfully handle your haters.

DIFFERENT KINDS OF TEARS

On 9-11, when you and I watched in horror as over 3,000 Americans plunged to their deaths, Arab and Muslim mobs in Egypt, Lebanon, the Palestinian areas – even Muslims in the United States – celebrated the massacre of innocent people working in the World Trade Center.

In his column in the New York Post, dated 9-14-01, Fred Siegel reported that several Arabs who were rejoicing while watching the destruction from the Statue of Liberty were arrested. He also wrote about Egyptians, Palestinians and other Arabs from Patterson, New Jersey, celebrated as they received word of the murderous attacks in New York and Washington. Why would these people dance in the streets?

Why would Muslims and Arabs right here in the United States laugh and applaud as good people were forced to jump from a 110-story building?

Because we as Americans are hated and let me tell you why we are hated: Because we are blessed.

Get it in your head right now that if you're going to be blessed, you are going to be hated. Decide to be blessed anyway.

Godly people are going to be hated and despised, and we need to know how to deal with it. If you are going to be blessed, whether it's on a national or individual level, somebody else is going to want to take that away from you. You will always have a group of haters setting their sights on you.

I want to talk about haters. A hater is someone who is jealous or envious. They spend all their time trying to make you look small, so they can look tall.

When you make your mark in any way whatsoever, you will always attract some haters. That's why you have to be careful who you share your blessings and dreams with. Some folks can't handle seeing you blessed. Just ask Joseph.

How do you handle your haters so you don't abort the blessings God has for you?

Here is something you need to know right off the bat: God knows you have haters and get this; *you are not allowed to become cynical, scornful and distrustful.* For these kinds of answers, God has a book for you to read and it's not the kind they sell at gun shows.

CALLING DOWN THE THUNDER

And it came to pass, when the time was come that He should be received up, He stedfastly set His face to go to Jerusalem; and sent messengers before His face; and they went, and entered into a village of the Samaritans, to make ready for Him. And they did not receive Him, because His face was as though He would go to Jerusalem. And when His disciples James and John saw this, they said, "Lord, wilt thou that we command fire to come down from heaven, and consume them, even as Elias did?" But He turned, and rebuked them, and said, "Ye know not what manner of spirit ye are of. For the Son of Man is not come to destroy men's lives, but to save them." And they went to another village.

LUKE 9:51-56

Have you ever been in a place where you wanted to call fire down from heaven?

Have you ever wanted to prove to the car in front of you that your insurance is better than their insurance? Or your mouth is louder than theirs, or your lawyer is meaner than their lawyer? Sure, you have.

We are all tempted to be like the disciples when we are hated. We want to call down the thunder and torch our enemies. Why? Because there is something within us that is surprised when that happens.

Secretly, we are all convinced we are cool and we tend to be shocked when someone else disagrees.

"I have had my fair share of mental pirates to deal with."

VENGEANCE WAS MINE

When I was 12 years old, I was playing in my little fort, when a man in the field next to ours saw me and called me an ugly name. I had grown a lot that summer. The pants I was wearing couldn't contain my increasing derrière any longer and I had a severe case of "plumber's syndrome" going on.

He made one rude remark and then another, and he just plain went out of his way to be ugly to me – for absolutely no reason than he didn't have anything better to do than to pick on a fat little boy.

This fat kid didn't have a big brother or anybody he could go to when people did him wrong, so at a very early age, he learned the art of "I'm gonna get you."

While that man was calling me names, he had no idea that behind my blue eyes I could picture burning his hay to the ground. The first thing I thought of was setting that man's field on fire and, in an instant, I made up my mind I was going to do it. Before he was even finished, I had determined what friends I would call and what time we would light the torches. It would be a beautiful thing.

Later that evening, my hoodlum friends had arrived to reap righteous retribution on the farmer next door. After having a whole day to think about it, I had decided that if we set his field on fire, there was a good chance that we would kill his cows. He had several beautiful Black Angus cows and I sure didn't want to endanger them in any way. I opted for a change of plans. The fires had died down in my head, but he would pay for mocking my anatomy in broad daylight.

My stepdad's garage was like a miniature Home Depot. Inside we found a case of white spray paint. From about 11:00 p.m. to 3:00 a.m., we chased that man's cows and penned every one of them. The sun would rise the next day to reveal terrible and derogatory statements written in white on the black hide of all of his cattle.

On Monday, I remember us kids on the school bus laughing our heads off as that poor old man was chasing his cows with a water hose. It is one of my fondest childhood memories. It was a beautiful moment, but it was not the right way to handle a hater.

THE FACTS OF HAVING A LIFE

If you can't handle being hated when you haven't done anything to deserve hatred, you can't handle being a Christian. Because God blesses His people and flips the script for those who love Him, the world loses its mind. They cannot figure it out.

He will cause the younger son to get the inheritance and the divorced wife to find the best husband in the world. He loves to make a difference through insignificant people. He will cause your house to not be touched by the tornado when every other house around you has been hit.

That does not make people happy. It actually makes people suspicious, envious, and hateful toward you. Why should you get a break when they don't? Why should you be blessed when they are not? Why should you have peace and joy when they're stressed out and anxious?

He will make enemies that should defeat you become defeated. He will take sicknesses that should kill you and kill the disease. He will take a head filled with pain and turn it into a mouth filled with praise.

When God stands up for His people, it makes other people mad. When you are obviously blessed, it makes other people upset. These are the facts of having a life in a world full of death. Know it and learn to deal with it.

PARTIAL EYESIGHT

When it comes to your personal haters, they see you blessed, they see you prospering, but they do not see what you have gone through, and what you continue to go through, in order to be where you are.

They see your glory, but they don't know your story.

Here is a great rule to go by when it comes to being suspicious of those who seem better off than you.

If the grass looks greener on the other side of the fence, you can be sure their water bill is higher than yours.

That's true in the natural and it is true in the spiritual as well. There is no such thing as a great man or woman of God without great affliction.

You cannot find an awesome person in the Bible, or the town you live in, who does not have a major malfunction they deal with every single day. When cursed people see blessed people, what they do not see is the price they pay every day to maintain that blessing.

A fat person might dislike another person who is in great shape, but they don't consider the choices the skinny person makes every single day to keep looking like that.

A man in a Volkswagen Bug might curse the lady in the Rolls Royce without considering the monthly expense of the note and the insurance on such a car.

It's really this simple: **If you want what somebody else has, be willing to pay the price they have to pay for it.** If not, change what you want to what you're willing to pay for.

It is the same way spiritually. You cannot have the ministry, relationships or anointing I have without going through what I've been through. Knowing this truth will keep you from being envious and hateful.

If you know these principles but your haters don't, here is how you can handle their lack of understanding.

HOW TO HANDLE YOUR HATERS

1. **Be a purpose-driven person. Remain confident in your purpose no matter what.**

When you have a purpose, you can focus without being distracted by your haters. Here's a great example: The Bible says the face of Jesus was set toward Jerusalem.

And it came to pass, when the time was come that He should be received up, he steadfastly set his face to go to Jerusalem...
LUKE 9:51

He was going to Jerusalem and it didn't matter if the Samaritans were on board or not. When you have a purpose, it doesn't devastate you when you are not invited out with friends.

When you have a purpose, you know who you are and whose you are, and it doesn't matter if people understand what you do or how you do it.

When you have a purpose, you're not going to be confounded when people you thought would stay with you, bail out because of the influence of somebody else.

Your purpose is not defined by how others think you can perform. If I know it's my purpose, I don't care what you think of the job I am doing.

I want to stop the car, get out and walk around this principle for a minute. If you are committed to coming to church, somebody will talk bad about you. So, you need to have some things settled within your spirit.

I don't go to church to make friends, join clicks, get somebody's number or because I am lonely. I know my purpose. I have been through too much to let anyone keep me from that purpose.

Can you say that about other things in your life? What's your purpose?

When I start getting upset about those who criticize or hate me, I forget I am a man on a mission. I forget how important it is that I am doing what I am doing.

Having a passionate purpose in your life is the key to dealing with your haters.

2. Know something about your haters.

The Bible says when Saul was anointed to be first king of Israel, the children of Belial came out to tell him he would never succeed.

"Children of Belial" is a proverbial term to describe worthless men. Here's the guy that is going to take everybody to the next level, and the very people criticizing him are, in fact, worthless, trifling men who are too dysfunctional themselves to get anything done.

We see the same exact thing happening today in the leadership of our country. At the time I am writing this, we are at war with Iraq. The President and his staff are constantly criticized and labeled as stupid by millions throughout the world. Just a few days ago, I saw several American actors speaking in public about the "utter stupidity" of our President and his advisors.

Shouldn't we compare our President's education and accomplishments to these actors and performers?

I could talk about President Bush, Donald Rumsfeld or Colin Powell and you really would be amazed at what I would show you. But let me show you the amazing credentials of National Security Advisor Condoleezza Rice.

Enrolling at age 15, Rice earned her Bachelor's Degree in Political Science at the age of 19 – Cum Laude and Phi Beta Kappa – from the University of Denver in 1974; her Master's from the University of Notre Dame 1975; and her Ph.D. from the Graduate School of International Studies at the University of Denver in 1981.

She is a Fellow of the American Academy of Arts and Sciences and has been awarded Honorary Doctorates from Morehouse College in 1991, the University of Alabama in 1994, and the University of Notre Dame in 1995. At Stanford, she has been a member of the Center for International Security and Arms Control, a Senior Fellow of the Institute for International Studies, and a Fellow (by courtesy) of the Hoover Institution. Her books include *Germany Unified and Europe*

Transformed (1995) with Philip Zelikow, *The Gorbachev Era* (1986) with Alexander Dallin, and *Uncertain Allegiance: The Soviet Union and the Czechoslovak Army* (1984). She also has written numerous articles on Soviet and East European foreign and defense policy, and has addressed audiences in at least 31 countries

From 1989 through March 1991, the period of German reunification and the final days of the Soviet Union, she served as Director, and then Senior Director, of Soviet and East European Affairs in the National Security Council, and a Special Assistant to the President for National Security Affairs. In 1986, while an international affairs Fellow of the Council on Foreign Relations, she served as Special Assistant to the Director of the Joint Chiefs of Staff. In 1997, she served on the Federal Advisory Committee on Gender Integrated Training in the Military. She was a member of the board of directors for the Chevron Corporation, the Charles Schwab Corporation, the William and Flora Hewlett Foundation, the University Of Notre Dame, the International Advisory Council of J.P. Morgan and the San Francisco Symphony Board of Governors. She was a Founding Board member of the Center for a New Generation – an educational support fund for schools in East Palo Alto and East Menlo Park, California – and was Vice President of the Boys and Girls Club of the Peninsula. In addition, her past board service has encompassed such organizations as Transamerica Corporation, Hewlett Packard, the Carnegie Corporation, Carnegie Endowment for International Peace, The Rand Corporation, the National Council for Soviet and East European Studies, the Mid-Peninsula Urban Coalition and KQED, public broadcasting for San Francisco. She was born November 14, 1954, in Birmingham, Alabama. She resides in Washington, D.C.

There is a lot more to Condoleezza Rice, but for the sake of our book remaining less than 500 pages, I will stop here.

There is a reason I showed you her resume. I want you to compare her to the caliber of people who publicly ridicule her and criticize her for being "an idiot."

A list of just a few of her haters and their accomplishments:

Barbara Streisand: Completed high school
Career: Singing and acting

Note: I would like to remind you that an actor is someone who gets paid to pretend they are someone important. They spend their entire life pretending to be somebody who is making a difference. Apparentl,y that becomes confusing at some point.

Cher: Dropped out of school in 9th grade.
Career: Singing and acting

Martin Sheen: Flunked entrance exam to University of Dayton.
Career: Acting

Jessica Lange: Dropped out of college mid-freshman year.
Career: Acting

Alec Baldwin: Dropped out of George Washington University after a scandal.
Career: Acting

Sean Penn: Completed high school.
Career: Acting

Susan Sarandon: Degree in Drama from Catholic University of America in Washington, D.C.
Career: Acting

Ed Asner: Completed high school.
Career: Acting

George Clooney: Dropped out of University of Kentucky.
Career: Acting

Would you lose any sleep if these people thought you were stupid? Do you think Ms. Rice does?

If I were her, I would lose no sleep whatsoever when these people criticized me. She doesn't have to address them or answer their criticism. She doesn't have to give them the time of day because, unlike her haters, she is smart enough to know the difference between what she is doing and what they are doing.

That's what we as Christians have to do.

Why should I let somebody who can't get it together keep me from having it together?

Before you listen to people, you ought to check out their history. If they can't get along with their own husband, don't let them tell you how to get along with yours. If they can't keep a girlfriend, don't worry about their criticism of your relationship.

If they can't even be faithful in attending church, don't worry about what they say about your ministry.

If they are not soul-winners themselves, don't worry about what they think about your mission trips.

HISTORICAL HATERS

It's not necessarily that they don't like you. They might just have a long history of criticism. The Bible didn't say the people who criticized Saul were Belial. It says they were the "children" of Belial. They had taken on the behavior of the people who produced them. They were just Xerox copies of the ignorant generations before them.

Let me show you one more way to handle your haters:

3. Know that you are in good company.

In a prophetic vision of Jesus being on the cross, the Psalmist wrote:

> *For dogs have compassed Me: the assembly of the wicked have enclosed Me: they pierced My hands and My feet.*
>
> **PSALM 22:16**

In another place, he wrote:

> *O God, the proud are risen against me, and the assemblies of violent men have sought after my soul; and have not set Thee before them.*
> **PSALM 86:14**

Jeremiah said a multitude had dealt treacherously with him. We could go on but know this: there are much worse things than being criticized and hated. One of those things is missing the good things God has for you. You don't want to miss the good things of the Lord because you don't know how to correctly deal with those who are against you. So, know that you are in good company when you are hated and persecuted. In fact, Jesus calls you blessed.

> *Blessed are ye, when men shall revile you, and persecute you, and shall say all manner of evil against you falsely, for my sake. Rejoice, and be exceeding glad: for great is your reward in heaven: for so persecuted they the prophets which were before you.*
> **MATTHEW 5:11-12**

Don't hate those who hate you and don't let them slow you down.

1. Be a person of Godly vision and purpose.
2. Know what you're dealing with when people criticize you.
3. Call yourself blessed, because you're in good company.

And dare to be all that Jesus Christ has called you to be.

SUMMARY PAGE

How to handle your haters
Spiritual Beef Jerky / Truth for Meditation

1. If you are going to be blessed, you are going to be hated. Be blessed anyway.
2. If the grass is greener on the other side of the fence, you can rest assured they pay a higher water bill than you do.
3. You need to be careful whom you share your blessings and dreams with. Some people cannot handle seeing you blessed.
4. God knows you have haters, but you are not allowed to become cynical, scornful or distrusting.
5. Don't hate those who hate you and don't let them slow you down.
6. Be a person of Godly vision and purpose.
7. Know what you're dealing with when people criticize you.
8. Call yourself blessed because you're in good company.

16

GIVE GOD YOUR MOUTH

SPEAKING RIGHT WORDS

"Communication is the heart of success. You daily words affect your success. You need to create a discipline in your life of speaking certain things at certain times until it is formed into a habit and becomes part of your nature."

DAVE THOMAS, FOUNDER OF WENDY'S FROM HIS AUTOBIOGRAPHY "WELL DONE"

I want to take you back several thousand years to boot camp. General Jehovah is explaining exactly how to be victorious in an unwinnable battle:

When thou goest out to battle against thine enemies, and seest horses, and chariots, and a people more than thou, be not afraid of them; for the LORD thy God is with thee, which brought thee up out of the land of Egypt. And it shall be, when ye are come nigh unto the battle, that the priest shall approach and speak unto the people. And shall say unto them, "Hear, O Israel, ye approach this day unto battle against your enemies. Let not your hearts faint, fear not, and do not tremble, neither be ye terrified because of them; for the LORD your God is He that goeth with you, to fight for you against your enemies, to save you. And the officers shall speak unto the people, saying, "What man is there that hath built a new house, and hath not dedicated it? Let him go and return to his house, lest he die in the battle, and another man dedicate it. And what man is he that hath planted a vineyard, and hath not yet eaten of it? Let him also go and return unto his house, lest he die in the battle, and another man eat of it. And what man is there that hath betrothed a wife, and hath not taken her? Let him go and return unto his house, lest he die in the battle, and another man take her." And the officers shall speak further unto the people, and they shall say, "What man is there that is fearful and fainthearted? Let him go and return unto his house, lest his brethren's heart faint, as well as his heart. And it shall be, when the officers have made an end of speaking unto the people, that they shall make captains of the armies to lead the people."

DEUTERONOMY 20:1-9

Now, I showed you this to make this point: Before anything else was set into order, certain things had to be spoken. The stage was set. The victory was assured by the words spoken that were directed by God.

BATTLE MOUTH

You no doubt have heard or read or know by heart the following famous scripture.

For the word of God is quick, and powerful, and sharper than any two-edged sword, piercing even to the dividing asunder of soul and spirit, and of the joints and marrow, and is a discerner of the thoughts and intents of the heart.

HEBREWS 4:12

You know the word is quick or "by the Spirit." You know that it is powerful, but do you know what it means when it says it is two-edged? The word here for "two-edged" literally means "two-mouthed" sword. What?!?

When God's words become your words and when your mouth becomes His mouth, a weapon is produced that cannot be withstood.

Out of His mouth comes a sharp sword with which to strike down the nations.
REVELATION 19:15

One of the most important strategies God gives us for overcoming anything, EVEN OUR MINDS, is learning the discipline of speaking right words. I know that people have been extreme in this area and a lot of junk has been taught, but don't throw the baby out with the bath water. You let God get a hold of your mouth and your life will change. As Bill Murray once said, "That's the fact, Jack."

LANGUAGE 101

If you're honest, you have come to the conclusion that you don't know how to speak right words automatically. The impulse to speak is always carnal in nature and filthy in substance. Just like any other part of our walk with the Lord, we have to be taught. If we are going to be taught by the Lord, we first have to be teachable people.

If you don't know what to say, you're in good company. When the Lord first introduced himself to Moses and revealed his personal destiny, Moses made the objection that he did not know what to say or even how to say it.

Read it for yourself:

"O my Lord, I am not eloquent, neither heretofore, nor since thou hast spoken unto thy servant: but I am slow of speech, and of a slow tongue." And the LORD said unto him, Who hath made man's mouth? Or who maketh the dumb, or deaf, or the seeing, or the blind? Have not I, the LORD? Now therefore go, and I will be with thy mouth, and teach thee what thou shalt say."
EXODUS 4:10-12

When you are real with God about your mouth, He will be real with you. In fact, if you will put your ear to the air concerning this subject, He will "teach you what thou shalt say."

A HOT HEAD

Do you have a constant conflict going on between your ears? Maybe it is time to bury your mental hatchet and make friends with your memories.

A soft answer turneth away wrath: but grievous words stir up anger.
PROVERBS 15:1

You will attract or repel wrath by the words you speak. This is true naturally, spiritually and it is also true mentally.

When you always have something ugly to say, you are going to attract the dislike, or the wrath, of others. Just like that, when not under control of the Holy Spirit, your mouth makes your mind a mental magnet for strife, trouble and conflict.

I am going to throw out some verses that may be familiar to you. Don't just look at these principles as just natural or spiritual. They also apply to the mental arena.

Right words will breathe energy and life in everything around you, including your thinking habits.

A whole tongue is a tree of life.
PROVERBS 15:24

Right words can energize and motivate your whole life including your thinking behaviors.

A man hath joy by the answer of his mouth and a word spoken in due season, how sweet it is.
PROVERBS 15:23

Right words decide which dreams live and which dreams die.

Death and life are in the power of a tongue. And they that love it shall eat the fruit thereof.
PROVERBS 18:21

Right words can get you out of mental trouble.

But the mouth of the upright will deliver them.
PROVERBS 12:6

Right words can bring mental health and healing.

The tongue of the wise is health.
PROVERBS 12:18

The bottom line is there is no way you cannot prosper by letting God get a hold of your words. What are you waiting for? Make a new commitment to God to be teachable in this area of your life. Right now might be a great time to repent for producing a septic line instead of a sword from your mouth. Get on your knees and fight like a man.

SUMMARY PAGE

Give God Your Mouth
Spiritual Beef Jerky / Truth for Meditation

1. The term "two-edged" sword literally means "two-mouthed" sword. Our mouth becomes a weapon when we line it up with the mouth of God.
2. Let God get a hold of your mouth and your life will undoubtedly change, including your mental life.
3. Speaking in a "new tongue" is a gift of the Holy Spirit. I understand the Spiritual Language that has to be interpreted but don't forget the incredible gift of simply being able to speak in a brand new way.
4. God doesn't just leave it up to you. He will teach you what to say, if you are willing to be taught.
5. Get God in your mouth, and your head doesn't have a chance not to have God in it. Get God in your head, and it will make the 12-inch drop to your heart and your feelings.

17

LET'S GET SMALL

"The unexamined life is not worth living."
SOCRATES

For if we would judge ourselves, we should not be judged.
1 CORINTHIANS 11:31

One thing that bank accounts, fan clubs, and lots of other things have in common is they tend to get small.

People in America spend millions trying to get smaller on crash diets and treadmills. All the while, they never consider a serious workout that will make them smaller in their own eyes.

The still, small voice as described in 1 Kings is not just a description of the voice of God, it is also a description of the heart able to hear that voice. If you and I want to know the heart of God within our hearts and minds, we are going to have to learn to get still and small.

Getting still is a matter of prioritizing your relationship with Jesus in such a way that you are willing to stop and smell the spiritual roses. That means instead of you getting busy with the next thing, you are looking to see where God's will and word is in the midst of your daily life. God doesn't just say, "Know that I Am God." He actually says, **"Be still and know that I Am God."** (Psalms 46:10) Prioritize God in the midst of your busyness.

COMBING YOUR BED HEAD

When you get in your bed, you need to train yourself to think on the things God would have you to think about instead of just going from one random thought to another. You get peace from the presence of God and if you are going to have peace in your sleep, you are going to get a Soul Invasion.

Let Jesus tell your thoughts the same thing He told the storm 2,000 years ago – "Peace, be still!" Put your mental remote down and quit changing the channel. Meditate. Focus your attention on the last thing God has shown you from His Word or in your life. Stay there and ask Him to speak to you.

There are some things God would love to speak into your life, but you are never going to hear them if you don't learn how to get still. This is exactly what the Bible means when it says:

Commune with your own heart
upon your bed and be still.
PSALM 4:4

What is God saying to your heart? You might never know if you can't get still.

LET'S GET SMALL

I remember the summer between the 4th and 5th grade. I spent a lot of time in the company of my good friend, Rick. There on his mother's turntable we put aside a KISS album and Fleetwood Mac to listen to Steve Martin's live recording "I'm a Wild and Crazy Guy." I put it on 33 speed and watched it turn around.

"Let's get small," he would say with animal balloons around his neck and a fake arrow through his head.

I remember trying to figure out what it meant to really get small. It was something I would not learn until I was in my twenties and walking with the Lord. There is no way God can be big in your life without you getting small.

QUESTIONS AND ANSWERS

A great question was asked more than 3,000 years ago as recorded in Job 4:17. ***"Shall mortal man be more just than God? Shall a man be more pure than his maker?"***

Another good question to ask in these days would be, "Shall a man be more anything than God?" This is a great question to ask Americans. When it all comes down to it, the answer to that question will be no. God has set things up so that man can never be more anything than God.

A FRENCH DUDE WITH A BIG HEAD (WHAT A SHOCKER!)

The famous French writer Voltaire often spent his wasted life and his expensive ink expressing his contempt for God, God's people and God's Word. When he so arrogantly wrote that his words and philosophies would soon be more important than the word of God, he got God's attention. About 200 years ago, this genius wrote this prediction from his library in Paris:

"I will go through the forest of scriptures and girdle all the tress so that in 100 years Christianity will be but a vanishing memory."

A few years after his death, the same library Voltaire wrote those words from was purchased by the British and Foreign Bible Society. That library was filled from the floor to the ceiling with thousands of copies of the Bible he so hated.

You are not going to be more anything than God. Voltaire has known that for a long time by now.

UNSAVABLE SHIPS

When the makers of the *Titanic* declared their ship was more durable than God. He turned their glory into shame and made their unsinkable ship unsavable.

When John Lennon declared the Beatles were more famous than Jesus Christ, within six months of that statement, the massive Broadway hit "Jesus Christ Superstar" was on the cover of Time magazine.

God is not going to let you be more than Him.

> *God also hath highly exalted the name of Jesus and given Him a name which is above every name: That at the name of Jesus every knee should bow, of things in heaven, and things in earth, and things under the earth; And that every tongue should confess that Jesus Christ is Lord, to the glory of God the Father.*
> **PHILIPPIANS 2:9-11**

It's inevitable that all of mankind will someday openly make God bigger than them, but it's better if you get in on that now!

MORE QUESTIONS AND ANSWERS

Colossians 1:18 defines what it means to be a true part of the body of Christ when it says, ***"And He is the head of the body, the church: who is the beginning, the firstborn from the dead; that in all things He might have the preeminence."***

Q: What do you have to do to be a part of the Kingdom of Jesus forever and ever?
A: You have to be married to Him; you've got to be His bride.

Q: What do you have to do to be His bride?
A: Through covenant and by His Spirit, you've got to be one with His body.

Q: What do you have to do to be one with His body?
A: You have to make Christ the head.

Q: How do you make Christ the head?
A: You give Him preeminence.

Preeminence is all about priority – Him getting big and you getting small.

THE INS, OUTS AND OVERS OF LIFE

What separates religious people from those with a true, ongoing encounter with Jesus is they continue to decrease while God continues to increase. You get small and God gets big. You are giving Him preeminence. Ultimately, if you're in the body of Christ, it's going to be in all things.

That means God does not just take priority *over* your marriage, your finances, your job and every part of your life – He takes priority *in* your marriage, your finances, your job and every part of your life.

Your walk with God is a lifetime of learning how to give Him priority over and in every part of your life. John the Baptist put it this way:

He must increase, but I must decrease.
JOHN 3:30

The understanding of "Christ in me" is a promise that I am going to get smaller and smaller, and He is going to get bigger and bigger. He is going to be enlarged in my life and I am going to be diminished.

The promise is that someday, I am going to supernova and Jesus is going to come busting up out of me in a way that doesn't leave anything of me. Until then, if I am going to be a part of His camp, I need to get this thing straight. It is my job to get small for the sake of Him being big.

SMALL PACKAGES

When I first truly caught this revelation, it was prophetic that the place I was camping was called BIG Bend National Park. Anything I had known of this spiritual truth flew out of my tent as God began to download something brand new.

It was the first time I had fasted for 30 days and I wanted to spend the last part of it in a tent, way out in the middle of nowhere. I had never sought the Lord in such a radical way. Consequently, the Lord showed up in a more radical way than

He ever had before. While reading the Word by flashlight, the Lord began to whisper something in my Spirit that would change my life forever.

"The smaller you get, Troy, the more I will use you."

He confirmed His Word by showing me the nine small things He used to do great things in the book of Judges. Let's do a quick Bible study.

YOU BE THE JUDGE

It is no coincidence that God uses the number nine in the book of Judges, since nine in the Bible tends to represent judgment.

Example: There are nine Biblical sieges against Jerusalem – each one a result of God's judgment against Israel. In Haggai chapter 1, God pours out His judgment on nine different things.

I could go on and on, but in any case, we find the mighty hand of God on nine little things in the book of Judges.

THE LEFT HAND OF FELLOWSHIP

In Chapter 3 God uses the weak (left) hand of a man from the smallest tribe of Israel (Benjamin) to kill the biggest King who had ever ruled over Israel. He did it all under the simple guise of a gift.

A KILLER CATTLE PROD

Then, in vs. 31, He uses an ox goad in the hand of a fellow named Shamgar to kill 600 Philistines.

STING LIKE A BEE

In chapter 4, God uses a little lady to encourage the people and lead them into war against a cavalry of 900 chariots. Her name was Deborah and the name Deborah means a "bee." She might have been a honeybee at home, but she was a stinging wasp on the battlefield.

THE MEANEST LITTLE MAMA ALIVE

In verses 15-17, Israel wins really big, but the captain of the bad guys gets away. He runs on foot into the tent of a woman named Jael. Now, Jael is the wrong housewife for Sisera to mess with. She knew just how to take care of him.

After running for miles, he is dying of thirst. She gives him a whole bottle of fresh milk. Seeing the warrior overwhelmed from exhaustion and a really high sugar count, she lays him down and tells him not to worry about anything. Let's read vs. 21 together:

Then Jael, Heber's wife, took a nail of the tent, and took a hammer in her hand, and went softly unto him, and smote the nail into his temples, and fastened it into the ground: for he was fast asleep and weary. So, he died.

I would imagine he did. A tent nail through the head tends to do that. Yikes!

A MUNCHKIN ARMY

In chapter 6, we have the story of another little person with a big destiny. His name was Gideon.

The Midian tyrants that ruled Israel were so bad that the people were forced to flee their homes and live in caves. There were no crops, no cattle and no wealth.

Verse 12 says it is during this time God raises up Gideon to be a deliverer.

So, here it is. He has an army of 32,000 soldiers when the Lord has him cry out to troops saying, "If you are afraid, you can go home." For 22,000 people, that's their cue.

When the dust settles, God takes them down to the water and gives them the famous how-do-you-drink-water-test. That sends 9,700 more of them back to mama and the kids. Gideon is left with only 300 soldiers.

It is with this TINY army God shows up BIG.

FROM MAKING FLOUR TO BUSTIN' HEADS

Forty years later, as mentioned in Chapter 9:22-49, wicked Abimelech rules certain cities with absolute carnage. He kills his own people, burning down towers and laying waste to strongholds.

In verses 50-53, he goes to pillage another town with a tower. As he lays siege to the tower and while he is trying to personally break down the door, a woman leans over the edge and drops a piece of a millstone. That rock nails him on the head and breaks his skull.

In verse 54, he turned to his fellow rapists and pillagers saying, "Quick! Kill me before I die, so it won't be said that I died at the hand of a woman!"

No cigar, Abimelech. We are still saying it today. You got offed by a woman! NA-NA-NA-NA-NA-NA!

A BOY FROM THE HOOD

In Chapter 11, there is a guy by the name of Jephthah. Besides having a train wreck for a name, he was the son of a harlot, rejected by the king's family, and thrown out of the palace. He had no potential, no promise for greatness, and no chance of changing any of that.

Yet, God rose him up as a deliverer. He defeated the enemy in 20 cities to rescue Israel and take back the Promised Land.

THE MOUTH OF A MULE

In chapter 15, God uses the jawbone of a donkey to slay a thousand enemies by the hand of a long hair named Samson.

Why would God use a left hand, an ox goad, a lady prophet, a tent nail, a tiny army, a mill stone, a common woman with no military training, a young man with no potential, and a jawbone to deliver Israel?

Because God was looking for optimum glory!

This is what He is looking for with us and He is not asking too much. That's why we must be willing to get small to be used by God in a great big way. He doesn't want to share the credit or the glory with anybody. Read His Word and let the Holy Spirit make this real to you:

> *But God hath chosen the foolish things of the world to confound the wise; and God hath chosen the weak things of the world to confound the things which are mighty; And base things of the world, and things which are despised, hath God chosen, yea, and things which are not, to bring to naught things that are: That no flesh should glory in His presence.*
> **1 CORINTHIANS 1:27-29**

> *For who hath despised the day of small things?*
> **ZECHARIAH 4:10**

> *Though thy beginning was small, yet thy latter end should greatly increase.*
> **JOB 8:7**

PAUL: THE INCREDIBLE SHRINKING MAN

Paul got smaller as he walked with the Lord. You can clearly see it in his writings. When he wrote his letter to the Galatians in 58 A.D, he started off his famous letter by letting everyone know his credentials.

Paul, an apostle, not of men, neither by man,
but by Jesus Christ, and God the Father,
who raised Him from the dead...
GALATIANS 1:1

Just a year or so later when he writes to the Corinthians, Paul doesn't put so much stock in his title or credentials. His perception of himself has changed dramatically in a short time.

For I am the least of the apostles, that am
not meet (worthy) to be called an apostle,
because I persecuted the church of God.
1 CORINTHIANS 15:9

About five years later, in A.D. 64, he doesn't even call himself an apostle. In fact, Paul sees himself as "least among the saints."

Unto me, who am less than the least of all saints,
is this grace given, that I should preach among
the Gentiles the unreachable riches of Christ…
EPHESIANS 3:8

Three years later, at the end of his life sitting in a Roman dungeon, Paul did not consider himself higher than anyone in the church. No longer quoting his credentials or touting his God-given titles, he wrote to Timothy, the young pastor of the biggest church in the world at the time. In that letter, Paul called himself **"the chief of sinners"** (*1 Timothy 1:15).*

PAUL HAD A CONTINUAL SOUL INVASION

You want to know how Paul dealt with all the conflict, persecution, peril, and outright hell he had to endure as an apostle of the early church? He got small. It wasn't about him. It was about Jesus. Paul learned to not think higher of himself than he actually was. This kind of soul invasion was so successful in the life of Paul, that he actually "finished his course" (2 Timothy 4:7).

It is true that Paul was decapitated in Rome. Still, he never lost his head. What a man. What a very small man.

SUMMARY PAGE

Let's get small
Spiritual Beef Jerky / Truth for Meditation

1. The smaller you get the more God will use you.
2. Still and small are not just the description of the voice of God. Still and small is the description of the heart able to hear the voice of God.
3. God is not asking too much when He wants to be glorified in us and through us.
4. God's greatest star players get benched when they stop making Jesus famous and promote themselves.
5. You don't really gain life until you are willing to throw your own life down for the perfect will of God.
6. Quit screaming for your rights and cry out for God's prefect will.

18

BRAIN FREEZE

A few years ago, I was in a 7-Eleven store with a missionary from Africa. It was one of his very first visits to the United States and he had not yet picked up on our lingo. He looked over at a Slurpy advertisement and asked, "What is a brain freeze?" Jumping all over this opportunity I said, "Here, let me show you." I handed him a cherry Slurpy, put a giant straw in it and said, "Drink this as fast as you can for about 15 seconds."

About 20 seconds later he dropped the drink on the floor and stumbled into the parking lot with both hands on his forehead. While he was convinced he was having a stroke, the guy behind the counter and I laughed so hard we could barely stand up. A few minutes later, my missionary brother came back in smiling and vowing revenge. He helped us clean up the mess. It was a real hoot.

I want to introduce you to a spiritual and mental exercise I call "brain freeze." I'm not talking about an ice cream headache or the cooling of the nerve in the roof of your mouth. I am talking about stopping a thought dead in its tracks before it becomes something else. I call that a Jesus-induced "brain freeze."

In order to get into this, we have to look at some serious truth pertaining to our thinking.

A WILD RIDE

Here's what's real: **thought progress**. A thought will turn into something else – a word or an action. Your thoughts are taking you somewhere whether you realize it or not.

As already stated, thoughts control feelings and, many times, feelings control actions. If we are going to be successful in our Christian walk – or any other part of our lives for that matter – we need to understand what we think on affects our entire life.

For I know their works and their thoughts.
ISAIAH 66:18

God even says that our thoughts and our actions, or works, are associated. You might need to stop and chew on this before you keep reading.

MOVING PICTURES

There is a true prosperity message, but it's not about giving God your money. It is about giving God your thoughts! Read the following verse:

This book of the law shall not depart out of thy mouth; but thou shalt meditate therein day and night, that thou mayest observe to do according to all that is written therein: for then thou shalt make thy way prosperous, and then thou shalt have good success.
JOSHUA 1:8

The Bible clearly states thoughts on God's holy Word will move you into success. The things you think about can move you into the victory you have always wanted.

The very same Bible also declares your thoughts can move you into miserable failure.

"And God saw that the wickedness of man was great in the earth, and that every imagination of the thoughts of his heart was only evil continually. And it repented the LORD that He had made man on the earth, and it grieved Him in His heart. And the LORD said, I will destroy man whom I have created from the face of the earth..."
GENESIS 6:5-7

The thoughts of humanity took humanity into the judgment of God. Because of their thoughts, God did not have to wait on their actions before He struck with judgment. Their thoughts made their actions inevitable. Do you know that until you are willing to let God change the thinking in your mind, you are never going to let Him change the outcome of your life?

FULL DISCLOSURE

God Knows Our Thoughts

Every proposal you consider, every scheme you contemplate, every image you imagine – good, bad, natural, or spiritual – is seen and heard by your Heavenly Father. God judges mental actions the same as physical action. If you don't believe it, let these scriptures invade your soul.

Let the words of my mouth, and the meditation of my heart, be acceptable in thy sight, O LORD, my strength, and my redeemer.

PSALMS 19:14

Are you consciously serving God in your thinking so that your mind is acceptable in His sight?

The thoughts of the wicked are an abomination to the LORD: but the words of the pure are pleasant words.

PROVERBS 15:26

O Jerusalem, wash thine heart from wickedness, that thou mayest be saved. How long shall thy vain thoughts lodge within thee?

JEREMIAH 4:14

...know thou the God of thy father, and serve Him with a perfect heart and with a willing mind: for the LORD searcheth all hearts, and understandeth all the imaginations of the thoughts: if thou seek Him, He will be found of thee; but if thou forsake Him, He will cast thee off forever.

1 CHRONICLES 28:9

Did you realize one of the ways people forsake God is mentally?

Let the wicked forsake his way, and the unrighteous man his thoughts: and let him return unto the LORD, and He will have mercy upon him; and to our God, for He will abundantly pardon. For my thoughts are not your thoughts, neither are your ways my ways, saith the LORD.

ISAIAH 55:7&8

Did you know God asks us to return to Him in our thoughts? This is not just an Old Testament issue.

And Jesus knowing their thoughts said, "Wherefore think ye evil in your hearts?"

MATTHEW 9:4

And Jesus knew their thoughts, and said unto them...

MATTHEW 12:25

And again, The Lord knoweth the thoughts of the wise, that they are vain.

1 CORINTHIANS 3:20

For the word of God is quick, and powerful, and sharper than any two-edged sword, piercing even to the dividing asunder of soul and spirit, and of the joints and marrow, and is a discerner of the thoughts and intents of the heart.

HEBREWS 4:12

You need a revelation that your thoughts do take you into dangerous places and God really does observe our thinking. He blesses or curses us accordingly. We need these truths settled within us before we can have a lifestyle that knows how to "BRAIN FREEZE" or halt ungodly thinking. We need to make a conscience effort to have true holiness of mind because we want a mind acceptable unto the Father. It is our job to allow the mind of Christ to be at work within us.

Let this mind be in you, which was also in Christ Jesus...

PHILIPPIANS 2:5

The point being, we are either going to allow the mind of Christ in our head or we will allow the mind of this world to be our thinking. It is God's desire that we submit how we think about things to the way He thinks about things. At this position, our reasoning becomes Holy Spirit led. That's where you begin to have a mind full of life, pleasing to the Lord.

Come now, and let us reason together, saith the LORD…
ISAIAH 1:18

A BEAUTIFUL MIND

In every courtroom drama, the central figure is the judge. He is the one who determines what is and is not allowed to be part of the record in every case.

The prosecutor wants to throw out a part of the witness' testimony as the defense lawyer argues why it should be admitted as evidence. At that point, everyone looks toward the judge and he either says, "I will allow it," or shake his head and say, "objection overruled."

If you are going to have a mind the Holy Spirit can work with, you need to learn how to judge your thoughts first. Judgment is not just the ability to discern what's good and what's not about thinking. Judgment is determining what you will allow and what you will not allow in your mind and life.

For if we would judge ourselves, we should not be judged.
1 CORINTHIANS 11:31

Do you have mental boundaries set up by the Holy Spirit? Things you will make yourself think about and things you will not allow at all? If so, you are fast becoming a faithful steward and well on your way to fully serving God in your mind.

SELF-AWARENESS

Here's what's real: You have the God-given ability to arrest every thought at any stage or you can advance those thoughts to another level.

Just because you are aware of a subject, does not mean you have to entertain that thought into advanced stages.

For example, you can be aware that you don't have the money to pay your bills without having a mental breakdown. If you entertain that thought and let your mind revolve around it, it will absolutely advance into imaginations more painful. Dreaded phone calls from bill collectors will send hateful feelings of frustration throughout your entire body. Recollections of "I told you so's" that either you warned somebody, or they warned you. Once you are there, your thoughts will proceed to endless "what if" and "what about" scenarios. What about my credit? What if my electricity gets turned off? What if they repossess my car? What about my kid's school supplies? Before you know it, your head will be full of strife and your body full of tension. It will inevitably show up in some nasty behavior or malicious outburst.

How do you stop all of this before it happens? Be aware with a real mental boundary that says, "I will not allow these thoughts to go all the way."

Be aware of a thought's potential and JUDGE IT accordingly. At the very moment you become aware of a thought that wants dominion in your thinking, discern if it is of God. Discern what the progression and outcome of that thinking will be, then make a conscious decision to allow it or not. This is a Holy Spirit-led process that, in time, can truly be mastered. As soon as you become aware of ungodly thinking, consciously – even verbally – commit your thinking to Jesus Christ.

"Commit thy works unto the Lord and
thy thoughts shall be established."
PROVERBS 16:3

The word "works" here means our actions. When we get committed to God in our mental or physical actions, He establishes our thought life.

HOTTIE ALERT

There is no way that a healthy male cannot be aware of a beautiful woman when she enters the room. This does not make him bad. This makes him a man. God programmed every man to be sight oriented.

A Godly man will struggle with this awareness and spend a lot of conscious thinking in extreme combat. Like the little train that said, "I think I can, I think I can," he chants the mantra of, "I will not look, I will not look." He ends up seeing anyway. By the end of the day, the scarlet letter "L" for "loser" is stamped on his spiritual forehead.

Knowing the truth about awareness can set us free from all this. It's not a sin to be aware of a woman's beauty. It is a sin to let that awareness escalate into carnal imaginations. There is a process involving choices here. We can stop that process by committing our thinking to Christ once we become aware.

Do you think Jesus was unaware of the beautiful women he was in contact with? He wasn't stupid, of course He did.

He looked, but He did not lust. He was aware, but He practiced the art of **BRAIN FREEZE**. He would not allow His awareness to turn into filthy imaginations.

For we have not a high priest which cannot be touched with the feeling of our infirmities; but was in all points tempted like as we are yet was without sin.
HEBREWS 4:15

Jesus was aware of the crimes of the hideous Roman Empire, yet He would not let His mind harbor hatred.

Jesus was aware of the corruption of the priests, yet He did not entertain thoughts of bitterness.

Jesus was aware of the sins of the people He healed, yet He made up His mind to maintain an attitude of love.

Jesus was aware that the very people He took care of would soon turn against Him and yell, "Crucify Him!" Yet, His mind was always full of compassionate thoughts toward them.

We must be aware of the things we are up against without letting those thoughts progress into something that separates us from God. We don't want to have a "God forsaken" mind. If at the point of awareness we commit our thinking unto God, He will show us the right way to think about that subject.

"Commit thy works unto the Lord and thy thoughts shall be established."
PROVERBS 16:3

We've all heard the question, "What Would Jesus Do" in terms of physical actions. Since our thoughts control our actions, it might be just as important to submit to the answer of, "What Would Jesus Think"?

STOP THE MADNESS

There has to be a place in our accepted wisdom where we recognize the chain of thoughts that lead us away from God. Once we recognize those mental patterns, we have to break a link in that chain and stop that thinking before it proceeds into a feeling, action or the very center of what we are doing.

With every bit of awareness, we have an opportunity to take that into further imaginations that will take us away from the knowledge of God. This is the place we go to war and freeze those thoughts before they grow into something that holds us hostage. This is what Paul is referring to when he mentions being led by the Spirit of God in 2 Corinthians.

Casting down imaginations, and every high thing that exalteth itself against the knowledge of God, and bringing into captivity every thought to the obedience of Christ;
2 CORINTHIANS 10:5

It is our responsibility to be aware of things without letting that awareness fast forward into sin. When Adam and Eve entered into sin, they did so through the fruit of a tree called "The Knowledge of Good and Evil." We should purpose to not have to know absolutely everything, but to know Christ in absolutely everything.

This is how we cast down imaginations and thoughts that want to replace or, as the Bible says, "exhalt themselves against the knowledge of God." We should become so in tune with what Jesus would think on a subject that we recognize and rule out ungodly thoughts before they grow into a monster.

Pray about it. Ask God to give you wisdom in your thinking. Get yourself educated in this area and verbally commit your mind to the Lord constantly. You don't have to mentally pursue every thought. In fact, you can't if you want to have real peace. So, practice the art of Jesus induced "brain freeze" and throw the brakes on progressive sinful thinking.

SUMMARY PAGE

"Brain Freeze"
Spiritual Beef Jerky / Truth for Meditation

1. God gives you the right and ability to stop a thought before it progresses into something else.
2. Thoughts progress into feelings, then into behavior.
3. The Bible says thoughts on the Word of God will progress into success. Thoughts separate from God will progress into certain judgment.
4. Until you are willing to let God change the thinking in your mind, He will never completely change your life.
5. God knows your thoughts and your actions.
6. God judges your mental actions in the same way He judges our physical actions.
7. According to 1 Chronicles 28:9, one of the ways people forsake God is mentally.
8. In Isaiah 55:7-8, God asks His people to return to Him, specifically in their thoughts.
9. It is possible to be aware of something without letting your mind go into active carnal imaginations.
10. It should be your purpose to not have to know absolutely everything, but to know Christ in absolutely everything.

19

MAKE A LIST OF...

1. The promises God has given you
   (It will keep you in times of trouble.)
2. Miracles God has done in your life.
   (It will keep you trusting God.)
3. The privileges and things you love about your life
   (It will keep you thankful.)
4. Prayers God has answered in your life
   (It will keep you praying.)
5. Favorite testimonies that make your "baby leap." (Things that have happened in lives of others that have taught and helped you)
6. The people God has put in your path to teach, encourage and help you become closer to Him and more solid in your walk.

This is your list of ready answers for a mind that wants to doubt the love of God for your life. It is something you need to make yourself remember.

I have more understanding than all my teachers,
for Thy testimonies are my meditation.
PSALMS 119:99

THE PROMISES GOD HAS GIVEN YOU

A great personal inventory to have when
you feel threatened in any way.

THE MIRACLES GOD HAS DONE IN YOUR LIFE

A great mental inventory to have when you need a real breakthrough. This is very important to have when your mind wants to give up.

THE PRIVILEGES AND THINGS YOU LOVE ABOUT YOUR LIFE

A great mental inventory when your mind wants to believe God doesn't love you. Sometimes, you have to make yourself be thankful. This list can help you accomplish that.

THE PRAYERS GOD HAS ANSWERED IN YOUR LIFE

An inventory of your successful prayer life will help you to be the prayer warrior God has called you to be. Sometimes you have to make yourself pray. This list will help.

YOUR FAVORITE TESTIMONIES

These are people and things God has moved through who have helped you believe and inspired you toward a deeper walk in the Lord. It will keep you convinced God is good.

THE PEOPLE GOD HAS PUT IN YOUR PATH WHO TEACH, ENCOURAGE, AND HELP YOU BECOME CLOSER TO THE LORD

A mental inventory of the family, teachers, pastors, authors, evangelists, singers, classmates and casual acquaintances who have made an impact on your faith.

Useless information concerning your brain:

When beginning to speak, unprompted words start as thoughts and involve many different brain areas responsible for memory, emotion and associations. These thoughts converge around an area of the brain known as Broca's area. It is here where we recall the memory of how to pronounce the desired words.

Important information concerning your brain:

A double-minded man is unstable in all his ways.

JAMES 1:8

Useless information concerning your brain:

Your brain is hardwired to recognize potential matches to familiar objects. This is how optical illusions work. According to research at an English university, it doesn't matter what order the letters in a word are. It is only important that the first and last letter are correct.

The rest can be a total mess and you can still read it without any problem. This is because we do not read every letter by itself. We read the word as a whole. Cool, eh?

Important information concerning your brain:

"Thus saith the Lord...For I know the things that come into your mind, every one of them."

EZEKIEL 11:5

Section Three: FOOD FOR THOUGHT

JESUS-DRIVEN THINKING THAT HELPS AND HEALS

The mind of sinful man is death, but the mind controlled by the Spirit is life and peace...
ROMANS 8:6

Two thinking caps you should be wearing at all times.

Three perspectives of life that come from God and keep our minds right.

Chapter 20: A Covenant Mentality

Chapter 21: A Kingdom Mentality

An old Cherokee chief was teaching his grandson about life: "A fight is going on inside me," he said to the boy. "It is a terrible fight and it is between two wolves."

"One is evil - he is anger, envy, sorrow, regret, greed, arrogance, self-pity, guilt, resentment, inferiority, lies, false pride, superiority, self-doubt, and ego."

"The other is good - he is joy, peace, love, hope, serenity, humility, kindness, benevolence, empathy, generosity, truth, compassion, and faith."

"This same fight is going on inside you - and inside every other person, too."

The grandson thought about it for a minute then asked his grandfather, "Which wolf will win?"

The old chief simply replied, "The one you feed."
AUTHOR UNKNOWN

In the Bible, Rebekah felt a great struggle within her body and inquired of the Lord:

"Why am I thus?"
GENESIS 25:22

The Lord's reply is the same He'd say to you and me today.

"Two nations are in thy womb, and two manner of people shall be separated from thy bowels..."
GENESIS 25:23

Feed your faith and starve your doubts. Feed your thinking that is of the Lord and starve to death your thinking that is cursed.

Here are some healthy mentalities every person with the right mind of God has to submit to. More than just philosophies or mere viewpoints, these mental perspectives can reveal the very mind of God and allow you to line up your thinking with God Almighty's thinking.

20

A COVENANT MENTALITY

Let this mind be in you, which was also in Christ Jesus...
PHILIPPIANS 2:5

It used to be when you shook somebody's hand, they gave you their word or when someone put their name on something, you could count on it. That day is long gone in America. We still shake hands, give folks our word, and even sign our name to things, but we do so with a loophole in mind. We keep a lawyer in our back pocket to file Chapter 13, file for divorce, or make an amendment to the paper we have signed because we no longer have a covenant mentality.

We stick to what we say as long as it's good for us and as long as we can see an advantage to what we are doing. As soon as we fail to feel good or see the green, the courtroom drama ensues (pardon the pun).

Our children grow up believing that marriage is a 50/50 proposition without any real understanding of true covenant. They come of age, rent a tux, buy a gown, and stand before somebody who will ask them some very serious questions.

Will you have this person to be your lawfully wedded?

"I do," they say and when they say that, they mean they do as long as there is something good in it for them. This is an American covenant and it's based on "what's in it for me?"

Will you love her and comfort her, honor and keep her in sickness and in health?

"I will," he says, thinking, *"As long as she is who I think she should be and does what I think she should be doing."*

Will you forsake all others and keep him only as long as the two of you both shall live?

"I will," she declares, secretly thinking, *"As long as he makes me feel the way I think I should feel and as long as I am thrilled about being in love with this man."*

They believe marriage will be a 50/50 endeavor. When they find out that many times marriage requires 100/0 they say:

"I don't anymore."

They fail because they are driven by feelings and not by covenant. This doesn't make them bad people, it just makes them guaranteed to fail.

A covenant mentality is an "all I have is yours, all you have is mine" mentality. It is a "sold out" mentality that says, "No matter what." It's the mindset God has for you.

Let this mind be in you which was also in Christ Jesus…
PHILIPPIANS 2:5

A covenant mentality will always produce integrity, reliability and character – always.

Our generation believes it's ok to cheat on your taxes as long as you don't get caught. It's ok to cheat on your wife as long as you don't get an STD. That's not how God thinks, and neither is it the way one thinks when he is or she is covenant-minded.

AN ANCIENT WONDER

The Chinese were so afraid of being invaded by northern invaders they built a 6,000-mile wall to protect them. One of the seven Ancient Wonders of the World, it was so high, no one could get over it, so thick no one could tear it down, and so long that no one could get around it. When it was finally finished, the Chinese went home to enjoy their new security.

However, within 100 years of building the Great Wall, China was invaded from the north no less than three times. The invaders did not have to go over it or tear it down. All they had to do was bribe a gatekeeper and they marched their armies right through its massive gates. All they had to do was find someone that was not covenant minded and the wall became irrelevant.

Many of the securities people have are just like that simply because they don't think with covenant in mind.

COVENANT GETS GOD'S ATTENTION

Covenant is the only thing in the world that will cause God to respond to you. God does not respond to poverty, to sickness, or to pain. If He did, every coal miner in West Virginia would be a Billy Graham. God responds to faith according to His covenant.

If your relationship with God is going to be based on covenant, you need to know this:

YOUR JOB IS TO GLORIFY GOD NO MATTER WHAT.

Whether therefore ye eat, or drink, or whatsoever ye do, do all to the glory of God.
1 CORINTHIANS 10:31

Look at how broad the Holy Spirit had Paul write this verse. "Whether" refers to action. Whether you are eating or drinking, standing or sitting, laughing or crying, buying or selling, traveling or building, or whether you are doing it all at the same time, **do all to the glory of God.**

This is a covenant lifestyle driven by a covenant mentality and it constantly produces selflessness and servitude. That's awesome Godly character. A covenant mentality says, "My life is not my own" when it is convenient and when it is not.

Do you know the main reason you can't get most people out of bed to go to church on Sunday Morning? Because they enjoy their downtime like the rest of us. You cannot convince them their life is not their own. It is not that they don't want to be fed the Word of God or worship Him. It is just very, very difficult to get an American to believe they are not in total ownership of their life. They lack character because they lack a covenant mentality.

Do you know why a lot of dedicated church goers will warm a church pew on Sunday, but cheat somebody out of money on Tuesday? Do you know why a lot of people will go to church on Sunday morning then spend the afternoon in a gossip cauldron? The reason is simple. They do not believe their speech, or their business practices belong to the glory of God. They lack Christian character because they lack a covenant mentality.

Whether therefore ye eat, or drink, or whatsoever ye do, do all to the glory of God.
1 CORINTHIANS 10:31

"Whatsoever" is very broad also. Whatever you are, male or female, old or young, whatever race, whatever denomination, whatever country you live in, whatever condition you might be in, in whatever circumstance, to God be the glory!

Let us forever wake up to that purpose! That is a covenant mentality. Everything we do within the body of Christ and within the realm of our physical body ought to glorify God.

Every one of us has a calling to glorify God. There are individual callings on our lives that glorify Him, but if we don't wake up to the purpose that we *are* to glorify Him, we can forget waking up to the purpose of *how* we are going to glorify Him.

There was a 19th century symphonic composer named ***Anton Bruckner. He*** signed every masterpiece he wrote with the words "to the glory of God." He got it. He understood his purpose.

Glorifying God means being occupied with and committed to His ways rather than being preoccupied with and determined to go your own way. The only way you can do that all the time is when there is nothing in it for you. Your actions are based on covenant, not on need.

The "Ins" of Life

In your public life or your private affairs, in your relationships, in your home, in your work, in your school, in your hobbies, in traveling, in your thinking; God gets the glory!

The "Ifs" of Life

If a person you love leaves or stays, if you have money or not, if a cause you support works or if it goes down in flames, if your plans succeed or fail; God gets the glory – not the blame – just the glory.

Because of this, my permanent theme in life is God gets the glory in public and in private. This comes from a covenant mentality. Hook yourself up with covenant minded people and you will be joined with people who will not split your church or stab you in the back. When people are all about the glory of God, their personal agenda takes a back seat.

THE NEED TO KNOW

There are certain things we know when we have a covenant mentality. Let's look at two of these.

1. A covenant mentality says, **"I have a place to go no matter what."**

Having therefore, brethren, boldness to enter into the holiest by the blood of Jesus...
HEBREWS 10:19

The holiest is the most powerful place. When I am in blood covenant with God through Jesus Christ, I have access to the most powerful part of God Himself.

2. A covenant mentality says, **"I have help in times of need."**

For we have not a high priest which cannot be touched with the feeling of our infirmities; but was in all points tempted like as we are, yet without sin. Let us therefore come boldly unto the throne of grace, that we may obtain mercy, and find grace to help in time of need.
HEBREWS 4:15-17

In Biblical times, families and tribes established covenants as an alliance against enemies. If I was in covenant with you and was attacked by an outside enemy, I could expect your help based on the covenant between us. It's the same with God.

Because of your covenant, you should **know** God is going to help you, fight your battles, bear your burdens and meet your needs. A covenant mentality will not allow you to doubt God when you need His help. A covenant mentality will not allow you to think God has abandoned or forsaken you.

NOT BOB, BUT A BETTER HOPE

A covenant mentality says, "I have hope no matter what."

And we know that all things work together for good to them that love God, to them who are the called according to his purpose.
ROMANS 8:28

Based on the covenant between us, I can come to these conclusions:

I am who He says I am no matter what.

I am blessed no matter what.

I am headed into better places no matter what.

I am loved no matter what.

I am a part of His family no matter what and it's not because of me. It is because of our covenant!

Your covenant with God through Jesus Christ, guarantees you are headed into bigger and better things – no matter what. It is not God's will, nor is it part of His covenant with you, that you should digress, worsen or decay in any way – except in putting Him first and laying down your life. You are now and always will be advancing into something better.

Living a covenant mentality will keep you close to God and keep you from running off the reservation. Living with a covenant mentality is living with a Jesus mentality.

Right now would be a good time to judge your mindset and see if it's based on covenant or on something else. God Almighty loves covenant and He loves to respond to covenant.

If you were to do a study of covenant through the books of the Bible, you would be amazed at how much stock God puts into covenant. Just look at these verses in Genesis alone: Gen 6:18, 9:9, 9:11, 9:12, 9:13, 9:15, 9:16, 9:17, 15:18, 17:2, 17:4, 17:7, 17:9, 17:10, 17:11, 17:13, 17:14, 17:19, 17:21, 31:44.

Get yourself a covenant mentality because that's what God has and it will change every part of your relationship with Him.

A COVENANT MENTALITY

Let this mind be in you, which was also in Christ Jesus.

PHILIPPIANS 2:5

21

A KINGDOM MENTALITY

A kingdom mentality says, "I am a valuable and privileged part of something much bigger than me."

...unto you it is given to know the mysteries of the kingdom of God...
LUKE 8:10

A kingdom mentality says, "I am a part of something that will never end."

...and of His kingdom there shall be no end.
LUKE 1:33

A kingdom mentality says, "I am in and I can never go back to what God has brought me out of."

...And Jesus said unto him, "No man, having put his hand to the plough, and looking back, is fit for the kingdom of God."
LUKE 9:62

A LAND WITHOUT A KING

It is hard for Americans to have a kingdom mentality simply because we have never had a king. The American culture is an independent, "maverick" mentality. We celebrate, and rightfully so, the rugged individualism that won the west and changed how the world does virtually everything.

Americans feel at home completely on their own. A true American leader is not going to wait for the approval of France to topple a Muslim terrorist regime. I like what Norman Swartzkoff said when France refused to help us in Operation Desert Storm.

"Going into war without France is like going into war without your accordion."

That is a classic illustration of the true American mentality and I love it. It says we have no respect for your little kingdom because we are Americans. You stay on your side of the pond, make perfume, and remain irrelevant while we change the world and make a difference.

"We don't need you; we can do it on our own."

While this kind of thinking is great for starting a business and winning wars, it makes for terrible theology and is doctrine reserved for devils, rather than the saints.

MISSION IMPOSSIBLE

Because of our mindset, the American mission field is a tough nut to crack. Say what you will, but I would argue that the toughest person to reach for Jesus may not be the bushman in Africa or the Hindu in India. The most difficult person to win for Jesus Christ I have come across, is the leathery, hard-working American man who pays his taxes and puts in his 40 – 60 hours a week.

He doesn't understand he needs the kingdom of God. Good luck trying to convince him. He doesn't believe he needs anybody for anything. He is completely convinced everything he has, he got completely on his own. He has never had to have a kingdom mentality and that makes him a very difficult man to reach for Christ.

When anyone comes to Christ, they come admitting they are completely dependent on Jesus for salvation. That He is God and they are not. These are the very first stages of a kingdom mentality.

BAD CREDIT

In the summer of 2000, our cooking teams gathered in a parking lot in Cleburne, Texas for an outreach we called "The Not Quite as Hot as Hell Street Outreach." It was well above a hundred degrees and we were cooking hotdogs and hamburgers over a huge barbecue. We had correctly named our outreach.

I had invited the pastors from every church in the area to help us lead people to Jesus and get these folks plugged into the body of Christ. OpenDoor Ministries is northwest of Joshua and nowhere near Cleburne. Since we were in their town, I thought it might be a good idea to get local churches involved.

Three pastors showed up that day and none were there to help. They were really there to check out what we were doing. Now in their defense, they didn't know us, so I can't really blame them for not inviting their whole church out, but one of them said something I am still talking about today.

When I explained we were rounding up hundreds of people and that I expected a lot of people to be saved after the concert, one of the Pastors asked me a question – and he was dead serious – emphasis on the word "dead."

"If we help you pray with these people," He asked wiping sweat from his brow, "who's gonna get the credit?"

I looked back at him stunned and said, "Jesus, I hope."

This is a true story and a perfect illustration of a lack of kingdom mentality even among pastors. That kind of ignorance would probably explain why that brother has 15 people in his congregation as well. He wasn't out there because he was happy we were reaching people for Jesus Christ, he was worried because we were invading his turf.

So, a good question to ask yourself when you are doing anything is, "Who's gonna get the credit?" Make sure it is not you, but Jesus.

THE BLOODS AND THE CRIPS

Because of our inability to submit to a kingdom mentality, we tend to see the church next door as our competition. The bigger church down the street or the newest denomination is not in competition with our ministries. The true competition of the church is the Budweiser Clydesdales, the Joe camels, the Rikki Lakes and the Jack Binions of the world that effectively sell people every day on the lie that they can find life in a bottle, in a bed, or in the chance for riches.

There is a church right next door to our church and it doesn't make me mad when their parking lot is full. They are reaching people I can't. They are making a difference and they are serving the same King I am – Jesus Christ.

LIVING A KINGDOM MENTALITY

This is how it ought to be in the church. The church of Jesus Christ should be kingdom of God oriented and not personal empire oriented. Don't ask me to participate in your personal empire because I want no part in it. Empires fall without exception, but the kingdom of Jesus Christ will indeed last forever.

And he shall reign over the house of Jacob forever;
and of His kingdom there shall be no end.
LUKE 1:33

My life belongs to the Lord. Whatever I can do to build His kingdom, I'll do it. If that means helping a Baptist brother with his outreach or helping a Methodist brother with his revival, I'll do it because it is not about me. It is about Jesus Christ and Him glorified. It is not about building something for me. It is about the building of His awesome kingdom.

The Body of Christ is not a worldwide organization. It is a living organism that miraculously grows by the Spirit of God. This body transcends race, language, culture, geographical location, and even generation.

It is not the generation that lifts up Jesus that is glorified, it is Jesus Himself. We are not building the kingdom, we are the building of the kingdom and this building doesn't belong to us at all. The Body is not ours, but the Lord's. So it is with our thinking. My mind belongs to Jesus and forever will be in service to the King.

A kingdom mentality keeps me submissive in my thinking and allows Jesus to truly be king, even in the secret areas of my thoughts.

The greatest of all commandments was made clear on a bright sunny day some 2,000 years ago. You remember the text.

Jesus replied: "'Love the Lord your God with all your heart and with all your soul and with all your mind.' This is the first and greatest commandment."
MATTHEW 22:37-38

Jesus said it then and He is saying it now: our number one priority is to love God. Not just in our physical actions, but in our mental and emotional realms as well. After knowing the mess that has been in my head, it is hard for me to imagine that Jesus would want anything to do with that contraption of flesh and thought, but He does.

He is willing to step into your thoughts and, piece by piece, item by item, remove the clutter and straighten out the disorder. He is faithful in serving us, so let us be faithful in serving Him.

May God bless and invade your soul.

BONUS CHAPTERS – SUPERNATURAL SANITY

At the time I wrote Soul Invasion, I was in my early thirties. I was just recovering from my very first church split and nearly suffered a mental/emotional breakdown. As the fog began to clear, I compiled all the notes from all the journals I had kept during that difficult time. Those journals kept my head in a right place. The result was this book. All the chapters were originally written for me before they were written for you.

I am now in my mid-fifties. God's goodness continues to impress, inspire, and challenge me to have a better and better thought life. About ten years ago, someone asked if I could finish a sentence about my testimony of Jesus. I was challenged to only use one word.

Jesus is my ______________.

Instead of feeling like I had to produce some theological gem, a single word flew out of my spirit and through my vocal chords: SANITY.

Jesus is my sanity.

Not long after, I preached a teaching series called "Supernatural Sanity." Since then, I have preached multiple sermons with the same title.

The following chapters are a late addition to this book and come from my conference notes from the past decade. It seemed appropriate in every way to revise Soul Invasion and add some Supernatural Sanity.

I hope this helps you to accept the invitation to have a right mind and one God can work with. May you have dominion in your thinking and peace that passes understanding. It's hard to tell the difference between supernatural peace and supernatural sanity. They are one in the same because they are both Jesus. I impart both to you through these chapters.

Troy

Section Four: SUPERNATURAL SANITY

Chapter 22: Why Snakes Don't Have Legs

Chapter 23: Displacement Theory

Chapter 24: The Road to Recovery

22

WHY SNAKES DON'T HAVE LEGS

The part of you that wants to play it safe is not the Jesus part of you. Jesus doesn't take shortcuts, sit on the couch, or avoid risk. Jesus is a warrior and His bride is a *warrior* bride. Jesus is attracted to the warrior side of you – the part that wants to fight – that refuses to give up. So, just like I told you in chapter 13, you have to armor up because you will go through dangerous places.

> *"Therefore put on God's complete armor, that you may be able to resist and stand your ground on the evil day [of danger], and, having done all [the crisis demands], to stand [firmly in your place]."*
> **EPHESIANS 6:13 (AMP)**

Just like when He sent His disciples out in pairs to prophesy, heal, and perform miracles, Jesus will send you out as lambs among wolves. He will make you stand for something you have no way of financially standing for. He will make you speak out when the people shouting against you are meaner, bigger, and uglier than you. He will cause you to help people who will turn around and slap you in the face and then Jesus will tell you, "I'm so proud of you! You're becoming the person I've always wanted you to be."

When that verse says, "having done all," that means you take care of everything you need to take care of so the rest of the battle is all about you standing.

The metaphor of standing is actually the subject of stability in Christ. If you are someone who stands, you have learned how to be stable.

I want to tell you, it's *so* important to the Kingdom of Heaven that you learn how to be stable. Why? Because it's *so* important to the kingdom of hell that your life looks like a ship being tossed about, out of control on the waves.

MAD AS HELL

Hear me on this: It is *absolutely* essential to the devil himself that you are demoralized. He needs you to be constantly frustrated and mad. As a matter of fact, the devil wants you to get so well-versed in being mad that you don't even need a reason to be mad anymore – you're just mad all the time. I know because I've been there and lived to tell the story.

With God as my witness, my beautiful wife Leanna has woken me up the same way every morning of our married life. She sings this little song in my ear until I finally give in and sing with her:

"Happy, happy, happy.
Happy are the people who's God is the Lord."

Why does my bride wake me up reminding me every day to be happy? Because she knows me. She knows anger is easy for me and I have a responsibility to stand against that in my mind. If I don't, it will lead to words and actions that will not glorify the Lord and kill my testimony.

On special days, after I was fully awake with a cup of coffee in my hand, she would smile and ask me in her sweetest voice, "So, who are you mad at today? I know you're going to be mad at somebody so you might as well tell me so we'll both know."

My friends, I am not lying to you when I say my mind has been a mess. One of the easiest ways for the devil to get you off track and kill your testimony is through anger. But, truth be told, the enemy doesn't have to tempt me into anger, and he probably doesn't have to tempt you either. The "in-a-me" is all I need to get riled up and twisting off from what the Lord has for me. Here's what's real: we can actually become highly skilled at partnering with the spirit of our own instability. When this becomes a habit, it's easy to lose hope because there is no hope in anger.

Brother Paul says in Colossians 1:23 that we need to be careful not to be moved away from the hope of the Gospel. It's one of those 1-2-3 scriptures and 1-2-3 is all about progression. That means hope is something you need to progress in. Do you know you can be a Christian, you can love God, and become unstable and dislodged from hope? All you have to do is let your mind go unchecked when something bad happens. You will have trouble "sure as sparks fly upward" (Job 5:7). There are a million reasons to lose hope, or become what the Bible calls being "exasperated."

Fathers, do not exasperate your children; instead, bring them up in the training and instruction of the Lord.
EPHESIANS 6:4 (NIV)

The word "exasperate" literally means "to leave without hope" or "to provoke to anger." There is a very real link between anger and hopelessness, and both lead to instability.

Did you know King David would speak from his spirit to his soul on this very subject? Check out Psalm 103 where he tells himself over and over again to "Bless the Lord" despite the awful circumstances in front of Him. He's talking to those voices of frustration and anxiety trying to overtake his mind. He's telling them to turn back to hoping in the Lord. David was intentional about not falling out or losing focus. He was intent on the Lord and refused to let anger turn into hopelessness and sideline him from his purpose. He supernaturally understood he had a calling – a purpose and a destiny that affected not just him, but everyone around him.

"The eyes of your understanding being enlightened; that ye may know what is the hope of His calling, and what the riches of the glory of HIs inheritance in the saints."
EPHESIANS 1:18

You know what? You always have to armor up to be able to stand because there's always going to be something attacking your stability – always. Most of the time, you won't even see it coming. Eve didn't.

TALKING TO SNAKES

In the Bible, the first attack we see against stability goes all the way back to the Garden of Eden. There was a beautiful woman named Eve, and she was the mother of everything. She was a supernatural reproducer and it wasn't just about having babies. Adam and Eve's job was to duplicate heaven on earth. Remember, they are in a garden – a guarded place they had stewardship over. It doesn't mean they had beans and 'taters planted in there, though they may have. It means there was a supernatural hedge of protection around the place they were responsible for. A garden in literally a "guarded place." Your mind needs to be a garden, but hold that thought.

In that place, they were so stable until one day a snake came to them. Let me start by telling you this isn't all on Eve. I'm being straight with you when I tell you Adam wasn't doing his job. Adam wasn't talking to his wife and reproducing heaven in her mind. Gentlemen, I want to tell you something: if you do not speak life into your wife's heart, there are plenty of snakes out there who will speak into her. Their words may sound life-giving, but they will surely lead to death. Something inside her will die just like it did for Eve.

So, everybody blames Eve. Eve was the one who bit into the apple but you need to know Adam was napping on the job. Eve had no business talking to snakes and Adam was the one who ignored the threat. Sometimes we men can get so comfortable, self-centered, busy, and we just get so single-minded that we assume everything is perfect with our wife. What's real is we have been on auto-pilot and the plane of our marriage is about to crash into a mountain.

Well, this snake shows up in the garden and he challenges Eve's stability. She was rock-solid because she knew God spoke to her. But the snake didn't challenge that. No, sir. He challenged God's goodness when he said, "Really, is that what He said?" Poor Eve was like, "Well, I don't know," and all of a sudden, this fixed place became dislodged a bit, until finally she and her husband were displaced out of the place God had put them.

Like I said in chapter 2, that instability caused the greatest act of abortion the world has ever seen. All of us died before we were even born!

Since they decided to walk in a curse, when God shows up, He defines the curse for the woman, the curse for the man, then He turns to the snake and what did He do? He took away his legs. That's a picture of instability. You have no ability to stand firm, ever. It also represents lack of righteousness and lack of self-control.

You are a born-again child of God Almighty. You do not have to speak to snakes. "But Pastor Troy, how do I know it's a snake?"

Well, if you're in your car or lying in your bed having an argument with someone who isn't actually there with you, you're talking to a snake. If you've just left an argument and you're going over all the "I should have saids," you're talking to a snake. If you're making excuses about something you haven't yet done and planning what you're going to say in whatever scenario that arises, you're talking to a snake. If you think you've been slighted, left out, or someone has looked at you wrong and you're imagining all the horrible things they're saying about you, you got it – you're talking to a snake.

SNAKES FROM THE PAST

When it comes to snakes and instability, beware becoming fixated on your past. It can poison your present and kill your future. How? Your fight for greatness gets replaced with a fight for preserving history and living it out over and over again. That's where it really gets ugly!

You can see how ugly it gets in the conversations you have in your head. Admit it. You think about something that happened in the past and think, "I should have said this," "I should have done that," or "What if..." You start to construct conversations in your head that, are not only practicing for a fight you will regret, they transport you back to the anger and hurt all over again. STOP IT!

From their callous hearts comes iniquity;
their evil imaginations have no limits.
PSALMS 73:7

All day long I have held out my hands to an obstinate people, who walk in ways not good, pursuing their own imaginations—
ISAIAH 65:2

The serpent wants to keep you wrapped up in your past so you never forgive. If you don't forgive, you will turn bitter. Once you're bitter, you are angry all the time and kill your witness for Jesus! Not only do you kill your testimony, you slam the brakes on your upgrade. Moving forward means forgiving those in your past by standing your ground. You do not talk to snakes.

TWO KINDS OF SNAKES

We give entirely too much credit to the devil for things he hasn't done. While a snake is very often the enemy, it can also be the in-a-me, which means it's an attack from within. Either way, it's a sandbox you don't want to get caught playing in because you don't belong there. You've been outfitted for victory. Check this out:

For the weapons of our warfare are not carnal but mighty in God for pulling down strongholds, casting down arguments and every high thing that exalts itself against the knowledge of God, bringing every thought into captivity to the obedience of Christ…
2 CORINTHIANS 10:4-5

The King James says, "evil imaginations." That's right, letting your imagination run wild and having arguments with people who aren't there to answer back are "high things" that will come against what you know about God and His character. They will exalt themselves by making you angry, bitter, suspicious, and eventually hopeless. Before that happens, you've got to kill that snake of the in-a-me. Lop his ugly head clean off!

You see, weapons are offensive items and the only weapon in the full armor of God is the Sword of the Spirit – the living Word of God. It is mighty for casting down of evil imaginations, arguments, and high things because it is the **truth**. When you know the truth about the Father, the Son, and the Holy Ghost – when you know how much they love you and have set you up for a great big identity, purpose, and destiny – you can say, "Devil from hell, I'm not listening to you. You are not the author and finisher of my faith. That is Jesus Christ and I'm not going to let My mind go where you want it to. I'm not going to fall for your lies about this situation."

Talking to snakes is bad and it will eventually kill you – your faith and your testimony. However, there is something worse and it's all about who you get intimate with.

SLEEPING WITH THE ENEMY

I love Samson but I hate reading the part in the Bible where he falls. He was born with supernatural speed and strength. His calling was to deliver his people from the evil Philistines who were oppressing the Jewish people and leading them into the worship of false Gods. He lays eyes on the Philistine beauty Delilah and he just can't help but become intimate with the enemy. Do you know what happens when you sleep with the enemy? You reproduce more enemies. It's the same with your thought life. You are going to reproduce what you think about.

If you think hopeless thoughts, you'll fall into despair. If you think suspicious thoughts, you'll be full of anxiety and won't be able to trust anybody. If you're angry or having arguments in your head, you've just practiced for a fight. You're loaded for bear and ready to take off the head of anyone who gets in your way. If you let yourself think God's not listening, that He doesn't care or that He's not really good after all, you'll build up a wall of anger that will separate you from the One person in the world who really matters. That's why what you think about God is the most important thing in your life.

Samson didn't understand this. Here God had blessed him in supernatural ways, but he couldn't grasp supernatural sanity and it cost him his destiny. The angel who prophesied to Samson's mama knew it when he brought her this great message:

For behold, you shall conceive and bear a son. And no razor shall come upon his head, for the child shall be a Nazirite to God from the womb; and he shall begin to deliver Israel out of the hand of the Philistines."

JUDGES 13:5

What Samson started, King David and his mighty men had to finish. That's not a good testimony.

UNSTABLE AS WATER

Long before Samson, another man with great potential threw his purpose and destiny away for a woman – one of his father's wives. In Genesis 49, Abraham starts out blessing his oldest son, Reuben. Because Reuben had let his thoughts become actions, his father ends up cursing him instead.

"Reuben, you are my firstborn, My might and the beginning of my strength, The excellency of dignity and the excellency of power. Unstable as water, you shall not excel, Because you went up to your father's bed; Then you defiled it— He went up to my couch."

GENESIS 49:3-4

Abraham calls Reuben "the beginning" of his strength, dignity and power, which falls way short of being the fulfillment of those great things. He then called him, "unstable as water" and declares, "you will not excel." The curse was instability and his instability was due to who he had been slee;ping with. There it is again. It's all about who you know privately. It's all about what's going on inside you that nobody else can see.

What stops progression in your life? Instability. Great instability keeps you from excelling to the next place. Instability comes from double-mindedness. You can decide what you think or you can just turn it all over to some monster. You can turn it over to Hollywood.

You can turn it over to Game of Thrones and let that worldview be your worldview. You can turn it over to your high school friends who are still smoking dope, getting drunk, and playing video games. You can turn it over to your whack family and let them decide what you believe and how you can live. Things are born out of these unions and they are your enemies. It is very possible to be a Christian who loves God but can't help sleeping with the enemy.

> *"If then you were raised with Christ, seek those things which are above, where Christ is, sitting at the right hand of God. Set your mind on things above, not on things on the earth."*
> **COLOSSIANS 3:21**

This verse literally means that since these things belong to you, you need to start going after them. To "set something" means to put it in a fixed position where it cannot be moved. Your worldview needs to be fixed. Your God-view needs to be anchored to one spot and here it is: "God is good all the time. His plan for me is good and I will fulfill my identity, purpose and destiny despite all the hell and high water of this life. I am an overcomer." Tell yourself that until it's true in your life. That's what King David did and it worked.

DOUBLE-MINDED DOESN'T MEAN TWICE AS SMART

In Psalms 16:8, King David says, "I have set the Lord always before me: Because he is at my right hand, I shall not be moved." He is saying, "I refuse to be unstable because I set Jesus before me. I will keep my eyes on Him and I will not be demonically bipolar." That's what double-mindedness is all about. When you're so unstable, you go after the things that will kill you. My friend, you must go after, and fight for, very real stability in your life. It's on you and nobody else to stand against the schemes of the enemy and the desires of the "in-a-me" in your thinking.

23

DISPLACEMENT THEORY

When it comes to living fear-, anxiety-, and depression-free lives, my friends, it's not just a matter of what you believe. It's really a matter of how you live your life. When it comes to victory, it's not about one thing. It's myriad things. It's about learning to celebrate the right things, and being angry at the things you need to be angry about. That's called the fear of the Lord – to love what God loves and hate what He hates. Amen.

I love what Graham Cooke says in his book, "The Art of Thinking Brilliantly." He says,

"You don't become a new person by changing your behavior; you discover who you are in Christ and your behavior changes accordingly."

That is displacement. You put something else into your thinking that causes the other thing to get out. If you want to get rid of fear, you don't work on fear. You work on love because love displaces fear. Love is selflessness. If you're scared out of your mind, the antidote to that is you just begin to give your life away. Lay down your life because love casts out all fear. (1 John 4:18)

KRYPTONITE KILLS

The kryptonite of anxiety is peace. And peace is not just you take a pill and chill out. Peace is the Lord Jesus Christ ruling and reigning in your life. He's called the Prince of Peace, amen. So, His royalty is attached to peace. In the places where Jesus is your King, He runs off your anxiety.

Just like that, the kryptonite of depression is hope and the goodness of God. These two things are Siamese twins. Hope is all about, "There's an upgrade coming. There's an upgrade coming." The goodness of God is all about His nature and God showing up and going, "Not today, devil. This is my child in whom I am well pleased."

BATTLING THE LIE

As you begin to reclaim your mind from the enemy, he's not going to want to give up that place he's had for so long. You're going to have to do battle with his lies. You're going to have to do battle with his confusion, so armor up.

> *There is no fear in love; but perfect love casts out fear, because fear involves torment. But he who fears has not been made perfect in love.*
> **1 JOHN 4:18**

Let me tell you something about fear: fear empowers and exalts the inferior but love empowers and exalts the superior. Fear is all about protecting yourself and surviving – that's what your carnal nature is all about. Love is all about selflessness and sacrifice. If you say you love your wife, then you have to be selfless and sacrifice. If you say you love your kids, then you have to be selfless and sacrifice. The opposite of love is not hate, my friend. The opposite of love is selfishness.

Matthew gives the cure to fear and anxiety.

> *"Therefore, do not worry, saying, 'what shall we eat?' or 'What shall we drink?' For after all these things the Gentiles seek. For your heavenly Father knows that you need all these things."*
> **MATTHEW 6:31**

He's not talking about not being responsible. He's saying to not become a survivor because survivors become selfish. Survivors cannot walk in the love of God because they only care about themselves. You need to become an overcomer.

THE FRUIT OF PEACE

Creative thinking comes naturally to a person who does not have anxiety. If you're full of anxiety, you're going to hunker down and protect yourself. If you're full of anxiety, you can't think outside the box. Why is that important? Because your box might kill you.

You get so use to living and thinking a certain way, then the Spirit of God moves and there's nothing innovative in you – there's nothing creative whatsoever. There's no courage in your life, there's no love of life, and you lose the ability to be creative by simply being full of anxiety all the time. The gift of God is stability. Check this out:

Every good gift and every perfect gift is from above, and comes down from the Father of lights, with whom there is no variation or shadow of turning.
JAMES 1:17

It's an amazing thing when God gives you supernatural sanity. It's a gift and gifts have to be discovered, developed, and demonstrated. Again, if you're full of anxiety you're not going to discover anything because there's not going to be any creative part of you.

This is not for casual seekers. This is not for people who are just remotely interested in something better and higher. This is for people who want to go *deep*. There's got to be something going on between you and the Father that's going to change your thinking and set you free, because the Father's desire and His good pleasure, Jesus says, is to "give you the Kingdom." He wants to give you all He owns and He wants to give you dominion. He wants you to have mastery in your life to enjoy and live a life worthy of His blood. He has paid a tremendous price for you to live this life.

JACOB OR ESAU?

When you were born again, you were born again with the Spirit – the resurrected Spirit of the Living God – living in you. Resurrection power and the Spirit of the Living God came into your physical body in the same realm where your soul is. Suddenly, there were two nations in you – think Jacob and Esau – and these two nations struggle. They don't naturally get along with each other. One *must* subdue the other.

In the Greek, your spirit realm is the word "pnuema." It means "the breath," or "the Breath of God." It's the life of Christ within you. Your soul is the mind, will, and emotions. In other words, your soul is your "Esau" and your spirit is your "Jacob." They don't get along very well. They're always fighting. Esau was born first, but Jacob, your spirit, is the one that receives the birthright – not your soul, not your "Esau." The promise does not come through your soul. Why? Because Esau was *selfish*, animalistic and all about survival. He thought so little of his family covenant with God that he sold his birthright for a bowl of beans.

That's what your soul does. It will always choose pleasure, comfort and "right now" before it will choose responsibility. Esau is the personification of that. But brother Jacob is a visionary. Jacob is looking way past the moment. He's always working an angle. That's your spirit. Your spirit is always working an angle, preparing for the future, and trying to work all things out for your good. Your spirit is all about bringing something of a greater depth and looking past the moment. Now, your soul must submit to your spirit, and I mean must!

FULLY MAN

Jesus was 100 percent God, but guess what? He was also 100 percent man and the Bible says He laid aside His rights as God and lived just like you and I do. As a man, Jesus was very aware of the different parts of His life; the soul-ish emotions and the spirit-emotions. Your soul-ish emotions aren't necessarily evil. They're just part of the human experience. You're not bad when you feel things. You're bad when you turn it over to your carnal nature instead of your spirit-nature.

Jesus knew and expressed emotion and He understood the difference between soul-ish emotions and spirit emotions. Because He was in human conditions and had human feelings, He couldn't help but be emotional about what was going on. However, He kept it in check by His Spirit. Why? Because He knew it was coming from His soul, therefore His Spirit would have dominion over that.

And then when it comes to your spirit emotions, you don't ever need to check those, ever. You need to let the Spirit of the Living God be expressed through your life, amen. That means you have to know the difference between your spiritual realm and your soul realm because sometimes you're feeling something that's coming out of your soul and other times it's coming out of your spirit. Sometimes, they're linked up. They're in tandem, and that's a powerful emotional place. You need to know the difference because your spirit-man *must have dominion over your soul* or you're going to be out of control and unstable. Your entire life will be about trying to pick up the pieces from when you last fell out.

How can you know the difference between your soul and your spirit? It's the Word of God. It's hearing God speak, getting the Word of God in your life. You *have* to know the difference between your soul and your spirit. What does Hebrews say?

> *"For the word of God is living and powerful, and sharper than any two-edged sword, piercing even to the division of soul and spirit, and joints and marrow, and is a discerner of the thoughts and intents of the heart."*
> **HEBREWS 4:12**

The Word of God comes into your thinking and separates life from death, truth from lies, and light from darkness. Why do you need to know that? Because your spirit is where you steer your life from. You have to speak directly from your spirit into your own soul.

King David would talk to himself all the time. He'd talk from his spirit to his soul. In Psalm 42 he says,

> *"Why are you cast down, O my soul? And why are you disquieted within me? Hope in God; For I shall yet praise Him, The help of my countenance and my God."*
> **PSALMS 42:11**

Sometimes, you just need to start going after your soul with your spirit. You need to make declarations like this: "My prayers are powerful and effective" because your soul isn't going to want to pray.

"God richly supplies all of my financial needs." That's Philippians 4:19. "I don't have to be in the despair of poverty." Why? Because God richly supplies all of my financial needs.

Here's another great confession to make to your soul: "I am dead to sin and alive to obeying God." When Troy Brewer speaks from his spirit to his soul, one of the declarations I say is this, "You better listen to me. You are not the slave to sin. Listen to me talk to you, Troy. You are not a slave to sin." Yes, I actually say that. I am not a slave to sin. Just because I feel like I am doesn't mean I have to go after that and you don't have to either.

I don't have to be afraid of any situation because I'm taking the Presence of God with me. "Through Jesus, I am 100 percent loved and worthy to receive all of God's blessings." That's Galatians 3. Take out a piece of paper and write down your own declarations and proclamations. Not only will your mind, will, and emotions take notice, Heaven responds when you declare God's Word over your life.

24

THE ROAD TO RECOVERY

THE UNTOLD STORY OF THE RESURRECTION

The Bible gives the most amazing account of the resurrection of Jesus. Though what happened at the garden tomb is what comes to mind when we talk about resurrection day, it's the account of the men walking on the road to Emmaus that is the real show stopper in my book.

Now, I've been to Israel numerous times and I can tell you from experience that Emmaus is on top of a mountain. Although it's only seven miles from Jerusalem, it's three miles straight down into a valley and four miles up on the other side. Kind of like life, huh? Hills and valleys, ups and downs. Maybe that's why the Lord Jesus decided to show up on this particular road. It would be just like Him to use this to illustrate His point.

So, this is the third day after Jesus Himself has been resurrected. Check this out:

> *"Now behold, two of them were traveling that same day to a village called Emmaus, which was seven miles from Jerusalem. And they talked together of all these things which had happened. 15 So it was, while they conversed and reasoned, that Jesus Himself drew near and went with them. 16 But their eyes were restrained, so that they did not know Him. 17 And He said to them, "What kind of conversation is this that you have with one another as you walk and are sad?" 18 Then the one whose name was Cleopas answered and said*

to Him, "Are You the only stranger in Jerusalem, and have You not known the things which happened there in these days?" 19 And He said to them, "What things?"

LUKE 24:13-19

Oh my! I want to just tell you, we all have a version of what God Almighty is doing in our lives and the Lord is listening. Just three days before this, Jesus had been on trial before Herod, Pilate, the religious leaders, and before the masses. But, here's the truth: Jesus was never actually on trial. Everybody else was. The leaders, the mob, those watching – they were all on trial and they didn't know it. Let me tell you, these two men walking the road to Emmaus didn't know it either.

Jesus starts walking with these guys. He asks about their conversation and why they're so sad. These bumpkins answer His question with a question of their own. "Are you the only person in town who doesn't know about all that's been happening?" Then Jesus asks, "What things?" And the brother who answers has no idea he's on trial.

You see, the Lord is listening to your version of the story. What story? The story of your life, your marriage, of who God has been to you from here to there, and who He is to you today. The Bible calls you a "living epistle" (2 Corinthians 5:2). You are not only the author but the book. The Lord wants to know what you say about Him and the life He's given you.

"So they said to Him, "The things concerning Jesus of Nazareth, who was a Prophet mighty in deed and word before God and all the people, 20 and how the chief priests and our rulers delivered Him to be condemned to death, and crucified Him. 21 But we were hoping that it was He who was going to redeem Israel. Indeed, besides all this, today is the third day since these things happened. 22 Yes, and certain women of our company, who arrived at the tomb early, astonished us. 23 When they did not find His body, they came saying that they had also seen a vision of angels who said He was alive. 24 And certain of those who were with us went to the tomb and found it

just as the women had said; but Him they did not see." 25 Then He said to them, "O foolish ones, and slow of heart to believe in all that the prophets have spoken!"
LUKE 24:19-25

Jesus' answer could also be translated as: "It's ridiculous you knew one little tiny bit of the story in the Scriptures and you thought you had the whole thing figured out. Now you think God has abandoned you and I Am not real. Because you didn't' have the full counsel of God, you didn't know all the things the prophets said. You only knew one thing that you formed a denomination around, then you skipped all the rest of it. Because you don't know what the whole Word of God says, you are totally messed up!"

Sometimes, Jesus just has to invade our messed up minds and set us on the right path.

"Ought not the Christ to have suffered these things and to enter into His glory?" 27 And beginning at Moses and all the Prophets, He expounded to them in all the Scriptures the things concerning Himself.
LUKE 24:26-27

Jesus is walking with them and they don't have clue it's Jesus, so He takes them to school. It's like, "Wait a minute! You act like you're surprised at those things. Did you not know the Scriptures say this and did you not know the Scriptures say that about the Messiah?"

Their response is so like ours today, "We never really looked into those things. We only knew this little part and we didn't see that part happen so now we can't believe anymore."

Then they drew near to the village where they were going, and He indicated that He would have gone farther. 29 But they constrained Him, saying, "Abide with us, for it is toward evening, and the day is far spent." And He went in to stay with them.
LUKE 19:28-29

It's very easy to just skip past this but you need to understand it's one thing to find Jesus in the Scriptures, it's another thing to **invite** Him in – to actually bring Him into your life. How do I know this? Look at the Word. It says Jesus was just going to keep right on trucking. It may seem like a strange thing, but it's actually not. Remember the storm on the Sea of Galilee when Jesus came walking on the water? The Bible says He walked right past the boat and would have kept on going if they didn't holler and invite Him into the boat.

VISITATION vs. HABITATION

It's about this: Have you asked Jesus into your life yet? You've seen Him in church and you've seen Him in the Bible, but it's not enough to meet Him in church and to see Him in the Bible. You've got to have Him in your life. You've got to invite Him in. I don't think it's just something you do at youth camp either. I think this is a lifestyle where you're continually inviting Jesus into your life over and over again with each new day and each new development.

Don't get me wrong. I'm not saying you can lose your salvation or that we have to continually get saved over and over again. I'm talking about a new kind of fullness, a new kind of dwelling – that the Lord moves from visitation into habitation in your life. That's a really big deal. Visitation is for acquaintances while habitation is for family – it's for the Bride of Christ.

> *"Now it came to pass, as He sat at the table with them, that He took bread, blessed and broke it, and gave it to them. 31 Then their eyes were opened and they knew Him; and He vanished from their sight. 32 And they said to one another, "Did not our heart burn within us while He talked with us on the road, and while He opened the Scriptures to us?" 33 So they rose up that very hour and returned to Jerusalem, and found the eleven and those who were with them gathered together, 34 saying, "The Lord is risen indeed, and has appeared to Simon!" 35 And they told about the things that had happened on the road, and how He was known to them in the breaking of bread. 36 Now as they said these things, Jesus Himself*

> *stood in the midst of them, and said to the, "Peace to you." 37 But they were terrified and frightened, and supposed they had seen a spirit. 38 And He said to them, "Why are you troubled? And why do doubts arise in your hearts? 39 Behold My hands and My feet, that it is I Myself. Handle Me and see, for a spirit does not have flesh and bones as you see I have." 40 And when He had said this, He showed them His hands and His feet. 41 But while they still did not believe for joy, and marveled, He said to them, "Have you any food here?" 42 So they gave Him a piece of broiled fish and some honeycomb. 43 And He took it and ate in their presence. 44 Then He said to them, "These are the words which I spoke to you while I was still with you, that all things must be fulfilled which were written in the Law of Moses and the Prophets and the Psalms concerning Me." 45 And He opened their understanding, that they might comprehend the Scriptures.*
>
> **LUKE 19:30-45**

What a rollercoaster of a day that was! What an incredible time that was! Thank you for bearing with me through the whole story because this is what God wants us to celebrate today:

1. **Jesus is there when we don't know He is there.**
2. **Jesus is with us when we don't know it's Jesus.**

I don't know what you're going through but the Lord has just arrested me and told me, "I want you to come against anxiety." The Lord has gotten me fixated on the importance of you being a man and woman of peace; not being overcome by the things of this world. He wants to remind you He's there even if you do not know He is. There are things in your life you don't have a clue is Jesus, but it is Jesus!

We live in very unstable times. Folks are losing their minds but you're not going to. That's not going to be you!

The guys on the road to Emmaus were so hurt and so sad, yet when Jesus came along they said, "But didn't our hearts burn within us?" How come they've got both of these things going on inside them?

Well, that's normal Christianity. That's what happens when you have the Spirit of the Living God living inside human beings. There's very real humanity involved. You're going to have issues. You're going to have fights. You're going to have bad stuff, even really dark stuff, happen in your life. It doesn't mean God's not there or that He's not powerful. It doesn't mean you have to live a powerless life. You're going to feel stuff and go through places that you want to make sense, but they don't. Welcome to humanity!

Jesus shows up to these guys and they're like, "We had hoped He was going to deliver Israel from the Romans and make Israel great again." And Jesus is like, "It is absolutely ridiculous how you have banked everything on something you don't even understand. The conclusion you have come to is that I'm not real and God has abandoned you. How did you come to that conclusion!? No!"

WHY AM I THUS?

I know I've talked about this in other chapters, but it goes right back to the story of Isaac and Rebecca when they found out they were finally going to be parents after 20 years of marriage. The number 20 is all about expectancy throughout the Bible. Well, Rebecca is expecting for the first time and things are not going how she thought they would. Here she is, a lady with no experience with pregnancy and there are two babies within her body who don't like each other. From the moment she conceives, these two begin to fight. Worn out and worried, she comes before the Lord and says

"...why am I thus?"
GENESIS 25:2

You've asked this question countless times. Why am I like this? Why do I have this battle going on inside me where my heart is burning but I'm also scared and confused? Why do I have this thing happening within my life? This can't be normal. And then God Almighty answers you just the same way her answers Rebecca – "There are two different nations inside of you and they will always fight." (Genesis 25:3 Pastor Troy Version).

There's an understanding I want to drop in your lap: Easter Sunday – Resurrection Day – was the greatest day for humanity anyone could imagine. It was certainly the greatest day the disciples could have imagined and they all felt like miserable failures. Sometimes, that's the way it is. Sometimes, God can be doing an amazing work in your life and you still feel confused. You're still not sure what's going on and you still feel like things are messed up. In those places, you say, "Okay, God. Why am I thus?" And He says, "Because you have a fight on your hands and the war isn't over." The truth is, because of Jesus' death and resurrection, it's ultimately over, but it hasn't all played out yet. We still have to live this life.

THE BATTLE WITHIN

You and I have the same questions of God that Rebecca had. If I am a man of peace, why do I have so much anger? If I'm a man of confidence, why do I have so much anxiety? If I'm anointed to have courage, why do I have so much fear? Why am I thus?

If you are a born-again child of God, you have the same resurrection Spirit living in you that raised Jesus Christ from the dead. But you also have inside of you a soul and a spirit. Like I've already told you, they're like Jacob and Esau. They fight.

You need to understand this: your brain was not designed to make you happy and stable. Your brain was designed to help you survive. It's always in survival mode and that's all it's going to understand unless your spirit overrides your soul. The difference between human beings and animals is that some human beings have the Spirit of the living God living in them. Animals do not. Animals do have a soul – a mind, will, and emotional base. Just like an animal following its instincts, the soul merely reacts to the environment it's in. Fight or flight 24/7. The thing that sets us apart from animals is we have within us something pure and holy that doesn't come from this world.

The good news is my soul can literally be overcome by my spirit. I can train my soul to be programmed according to the Word of God and the Spirit of the Living God living inside me. I can actually have the mind of Christ.

When your emotions are out of whack and there's something you haven't dealt with in years and it comes back around and bites you – this is common among human beings. But let me tell you what's not common: people who stick with God through all those things. Those people have the power of the Holy Spirit within their life and they might miss it here or there, but they finally get it. They finally learn how to overcome.

Friends, you have to overcome your mind, will, and emotions. Yes, the animalistic nature of you that wants to survive is a valuable tool, but it's also a destroyer if the Spirit of God does not control your soul.

THE CURE FOR DEPRESSION

You have to learn how to serve God in your emotional life and not fall into depression or hopelessness. I'm talking about the power of adoration. Adoration is an emotional response to the love of God. Adoration involves joy, happiness, and laughter. It's an intentional passion for Jesus. It's like when the psalmist said,

> *"I was glad when they said to me, 'Let us go to the house of the Lord!'"*
> **PSALM 122:1**

That's an intentional posture where your spirit intentionally tells your soul to get ready because it's going to worship the Lord today! Sometimes, I do not feel joyful, but I do feel the Lord. He has not abandoned me. The Spirit of God is with me and He's with you too. He has not abandoned you if something in your life is not perfect.

It's about building up a track record. "But Pastor Troy, you don't know how many times I've been stabbed in the back. You don't know how much hate mail I get or how many failures and disappointments I have. Terrible things have been said and done to me. There are so many things I wish I had but I don't have those things." That's not your track record.

Your track record is this: when I seek Him, I find Him. When I ask, He answers. When I knock, He opens the door unto me. Have a track record of dreams, visions, and mysteries. Have a track record of miracles and wonders within your life, and get excited about that!

BEWARE THE CHOSEN FROZEN

Now, religion doesn't want you to get excited about anything because you're liable to get out of their control. Religion is always about control. Always. It doesn't matter what brand it comes in – Christian, Muslim, Hindu, Buddhist, New Age religion – it always has an agenda to control you. That's why if you start to get a little bit excited during praise and worship, Sister Suzy Rottenheart will come over and say, "We don't do that here. You're making us nervous." Or "That's not our form of expression during worship and if you're going to be here, you need to look and act just like we do behind our stained glass windows."

Well, Sister Suzy, I didn't wake up this morning needing your approval. When did I need your approval to worship my God? When did I need a fan club? When did I need an amen-corner to tell me it's okay to be excited about Jesus? I don't and I never will – and neither do you, my friend!

You know, when that woman in Luke 7:37 came busting in with the alabaster box and poured perfume all over King Jesus' feet, and used her tears and her hair to wash them, that was highly inappropriate in that society. Nonetheless, it was an intentional posture. That was how she was worshipping God. She was worshipping the Lord prophetically, emotionally and with her wealth. She didn't care what anybody thought. She was going to love on her Jesus. The reason you and I get attacked by fear, anxiety, and worry about offending social norms is because the enemy wants to derail us from an emotional expression toward King Jesus. Why? Because it is powerful.

This belongs to us just like it belonged to those men on the road to Emmaus who said, "Did not our hearts burn within us as He walked with us by the way?" The Bible says you enter His gates with thanksgiving and praise. Learn to have a disciplined emotional response when you come before the Lord based upon the Word of God. I say things like this:

My prayers are powerful and effective. (2 Corinthians 5:21 and James 5:16)

God richly supplies all my financial needs. (Philippians 4:19)

I am dead to sin and alive to obeying God. (Romans 6:11)

I live under supernatural protection. (Psalm 91)

I walk in ever-increasing health. (Isaiah 53-3-5)

I prosper in all my relationships. (Luke 2:52)

I consistently bring God encounters to other people. (Mark 16:17-18)

Through Jesus, I am 100 percent loved and worthy to receive all of God's blessings. (Galatians 3:1-5)

Each of my family members is wonderfully blessed and called to radically love Jesus. (Acts 16:30-31)

I laugh when I hear a lie from the devil. (Psalm 2:2-4)

I'm bound and determined to not just bring my mind and spirit, but to bring my emotions into this thing to truly serve God the way He deserves. It also helps me not become a psychotic basket case. It reminds me of when you know someone is coming to your house, you fix up their room for them. You do everything you can do to make it nice, warm and inviting for the person visiting you. If you're going to seek the Lord, you bring everything you have to the table and watch how God Almighty responds to that. He'll show up for you the same as He shows up for me.

My friend, if you've been asking the Lord, "Why am I thus," it's okay. You're going to be okay. You really and truly are because you're going to pursue Jesus. You're going to turn your heart, your mind, and your emotions over to His mind, His heart, and His will for your life. God will call it beautiful. He does not hate your humanity. He loves your messed-up humanity: "For God so loved the world…"

My friend, that means you. He loves you, messed up mind and all. You are perfect for the Kingdom – you really are. God can use people like you and me. Just you watch and see.

THANK YOU AND ACKNOWLEDGMENTS

Debbie and Richmond Caldwell
Debbie, your help in editing and working with this book was timed completely by the Holy Spirit. Thank you so much.

Richmond, when you offered to bring Leanna and I with you to invade your vacation, I knew that I would have a week to finish this book. Thank you so much for your personal friendship and know that God used your blessing to help me wrap this work up in a way I hope will benefit others.

Kyp Shillam
Thank you for putting the editing polish on this work of heart.

Tommy Owen
You're such a pro! Your design work and graphics are always next level because that's how you roll (www.TommyOwenDesign.com).

William Edward Brewer
Dad, I started this book in the stormiest and most difficult time of my life, determined to get out of the mess that was trying to kill me. Thank you for standing with me, loving me, and helping me through that dark and dreadful year.

Seeing how you loved me, and stood for me in 2011 caused me to see my Heavenly Father standing with me and loving me. 2012 was amazing and now 2013 is ten levels higher in every way because of who you are, sir.

Sure do love you, Pop.

– Troy

CONTACT THE AUTHOR

Email:
tbrewer@troybrewer.com

Snail mail:
301 S. Dobson St.,
Burleson, TX 76028

Church Website:
OpendoorExperience.com

Ministry Websites:
TroyBrewer.com
AnswerInternational.org
TroyBrewer.TV

Spark Website:
SparkWorldwide.org
Facebook: @pstroybrewer
Twitter: @pstroybrewer

24-hour prayer, resource and sponsorship hotline:
1.877.413.0888

Troy speaks at a variety of conferences and churches, both domestically and internationally. If you would like to inquire into his availability for ministry, you can contact him through the above information or call the OpenDoor Church offices at 817-295-7671.

OTHER BOOKS

BY TROY BREWER

Fresh From The Brewer
Volume I.

Fresh From The Brewer
Volume Ii.

Best Of The Brewer

Good Overcomes
Evil

Looking Up

Numbers That
Preach

Miracles With
A Message

Living Life /
Forward

Daily Transformation

NOTES